DAY 7

FOR WORK, REST, OR PLAY

JOEL BIERMANN

~~Our~~ the reason ~~for~~ we ~~to~~

~~Living~~ Live the

Down & Out Life-

Delighting in the Down &

Out L

~~Day~~ 7: Embracing God's

Sabbath and

work, rest, or

Re-thinking S

Joyfully living

the Down and Out

Life and the Joy

it Brings

Sabbath and the

of Exist

The Point of it

~~Day 7: God's Plan Design for the Down and Out Gift~~

Your Reason for

A Down

Life

Sabbath Work: Re-Thinkin

Rest

~~God's Plan~~ for

Receiving G

WHAT READERS ARE SAYING . . .

Prepare for a worldview reevaluation. Sabbath isn't about a relegated day of the week—it's about a lifestyle that receives God's good gifts and does life the way He intends. It means being right with God and being right with His creation. It means living in tune with the reality of God's world grounded in truth, goodness, and beauty. At times, that includes work; other times, it includes leisure or play. But in all of it, it means a worshipful delight in that which we have received from God—the *vita receptiva*.

—Dr. Nathan Olson, professor, Free Lutheran Bible College and Seminary, Plymouth, Minnesota

Dr. Biermann moves the reader from what he knows to what he thinks he knows to what he needs to know about remembering the Sabbath day. In lucid fashion, Biermann displays how it is that rest, work, leisure, and other topics are related to living a life in accordance with the Third Commandment. The book is personal, in that you will see your life from God's perspective. With God's blessing, the reader will gain a new appreciation and increased joy for whom God has made him to be and how God would have him live and rejoice in life that is shaped by day seven.

—Rev. W. Max Mons, STM, pastor, St. Paul's Lutheran Chapel, Iowa City, Iowa; first vice president, LCMS Iowa District East; chairman, board of regents, Concordia Seminary

Dr. Biermann has wonderfully unpackaged the Sabbath, showing how day seven is truly foundational for our lives. From the beginning, each chapter reveals connections that help us see the gracious purposes our Lord has intended for every one of us. In an era when many are feeling frustrated by the complexities and distractions of postmodern life, this book brings clarity and joy. You will see the Lord's Day—not just the time of worship but the whole day—in a new way and be very glad you did. I will be returning to this volume and incorporating its wisdom into my life and teaching.

—Phillip Magness, cantor and LCMS missionary in Africa

WHAT READERS ARE SAYING . . .

The Sabbath was made for you, and yet what have you done with it? Be restored in the Sabbath and in the very purpose of your life in this wonderful and insightful book. Biermann shows that we are not machines that switch off and on but are embodied souls and living organisms made within a divine order that is good, true, and beautiful. In an age of alienation and displacement, this book will help you find your true home and place in the eternal kingdom of the Lord of the Sabbath.

—**Thomas Pietsch,** pastor, Bethlehem Lutheran Church, Adelaide, Australia; PhD candidate, Australian Catholic University

In his doctrine of vocation, Luther takes his theology out of the ivory tower and puts it into practice in the daily lives of Christians. Joel Biermann's *Day 7* helps Christians understand Luther's explanation of Sabbath rest and the relationship of work, rest, and leisure in their daily lives. His treatment of the receptive life is particularly helpful for individuals to appreciate God's gifts and serve their neighbors in love.

—**Rev. Dr. R. Lee Hagan,** president, Missouri District of The Lutheran Church—Missouri Synod

FOR

Oliver, Titus, Hadley, Jude,
Benton, Grey, Adelaide, Dietrich,
Edmund, Genevieve, and Otto;
never stop playing.

Published by Concordia Publishing House
3558 S. Jefferson Ave., St. Louis, MO 63118-3968
1-800-325-3040 · cph.org

1 2 3 4 5 6 7 8 9 10 33 32 31 30 29 28 27 26 25 24

TABLE OF CONTENTS

INTRODUCTION 8

1. SABBATH IN THE CATECHISM 20

2. SABBATH IN THE BIBLE 42

3. WORK 78

4. LEISURE 110

5. THE RECEPTIVE LIFE 144

6. SLEEP AND PLAY 188

7. CONCLUSION: LIVING THE RECEPTIVE LIFE 222

INTRODUCTION

This book is about your life.

That is, of course, a claim that is at once both remarkably presumptive and wholly ambiguous. I'll address the second problem first. This is not a scientific book exploring the inner workings of the literal anatomy, psychology, and physiology that shape and direct your life—though all of those thoroughly biological and physical factors of your humanity are certainly relevant to your life. This book is not a self-help book; nevertheless, I do hope that it will prove helpful to you, the reader, and those you know. What follows is intended to be quite practical, but it is certainly not a practical guidebook that will lead you with step-by-step instructions to unravel a complicated problem or resolve a difficult situation in your life. It is not a manual that if followed will produce a wonderful new life overflowing with prosperity and joy. No, this is simply a book about the reality of your life, which you encounter every morning after morning after morning. It's about the mundane routines and demands of a complete life from the long sometimes listless days of childhood to the frenetic busy-ness of youth, the settled and sapping responsibilities of adulthood, and the empty spaces of old age. This book is about the whole of life—the normal things of normal life that shape and animate the reality you daily encounter—your normal things in your normal life. It does not matter who you are, where you live, how long you have lived, what you have experienced, what you believe, or what you do, have done, or will do. This book is about you and the reality that is your life.

THE PLAN AND THE QUESTION

As I already noted, this sounds exceedingly presumptive and not a little immodest. Only a single sentence into the introduction and already I have promised far more than seems possible for one slim book to deliver. On top of that, by making such a sweeping claim without caveat, disclaimer, or the standard academic hedging of bets, I rather blatantly and foolishly expose myself to the charge of being just that sort of know-it-all, shamelessly arrogant, insufferable professor who is altogether too sure (not to mention *full*) of himself. But, aware of the skepticism and ridicule it may provoke, I stand by my claim. This book is about you, no matter who you are. It is about you and your life because this book is about the essential, core truths of what it means to be human. These defining truths inescapably apply to every single human being ever to walk this planet, which certainly includes you. I don't have to meet you, hear your life story, or understand your unique viewpoints or feelings to be able to tell you what you need to know about your life. I already know everything that I need to know in order to tell you all that you need to know. And no, it is not arrogance or even ignorance that drives me to make such a bold claim. It is not because having now lived for six-plus decades has given me some spectacular insight into the secret of life that I am now brazen enough to divulge. No, I can tell you and every other human being about your life because what I intend to tell you is what God tells you. That's the source of my confidence. What I will unfold in the pages that follow are not my ideas. They are God's ideas.

Actually, I write this short book with a healthy sense of trepidation and hesitation. I've written a fair amount in my life: academic papers laden with footnotes designed to bolster and propel a carefully crafted and nuanced argument, books exploring what seemed to me to be significant theological ideas

I thought needed to be unpacked and understood, and sermons . . . hundreds and hundreds of sermons. But this book is like none of those. This is not a book for the academy, but for everyone. It is about your life, after all, and since the "you" is every person, it should be written so that every person can read it. I will try to do that. That means that this book will have more in common with a sermon than with a treatise for the academy. But it will also be thicker, more speculative, and more laden with detail and, I hope, legitimately thought-provoking ideas than what is expected and accepted in a typical sermon. Like a sermon, I will delve into the Bible itself and explore vital truths that are revealed there, but I'll also spend time thinking about some old and important ideas from philosophy and even explore some issues that touch on questions of culture and sociology. This is not at all, then, an anti-academic rant. Indeed, my place on the edge of the academy (at least, that's where I locate myself as a seminary professor) will undoubtedly shape all that follows; that can't be helped. I hope, though, to make that influence an enhancement and not a burden to be endured.

I am a seminary professor and have served with profound gratitude and daily delight in that capacity for more than twenty years of my life. In my case, it is without question the seminary (that is, the theological) part of the descriptor that is most significant. I have been stamped far more by the truths, claims, and practices of the church than by the world of the university or the academy. That, of course, accounts for the file folders full of sermons that litter my personal archives. That truth also accounts for the unbridled confidence exhibited as I began this introduction. I haven't forgotten my purpose. This book is not an academic paper, and neither is it my personal reflection or memoir. It is about you and your life and the profound meaning that is embedded in your life and how that meaning should animate all the activities of your life. It is about the purpose and meaning of your *whole* life. I can write about such intimately personal things in your world with confidence, not because I have scholarly detachment or unbounded intellectual abilities, but simply because I have a theological commitment. Far more than a professor of the academy, I am a pastor of Christ's church. That is the reality that shapes all I think, teach, say, and do—at least, that is the reality that should shape all of those things. While I routinely and stupendously fall short of the ideal, I nevertheless understand my obligation to speak God's truth and to pass on what I have been given. That's what drives my effort in the book that follows. And that's why I can speak with such confidence and, at times, even specificity to you about your life.

What I write is what I have been given to write. It is God's truth. Of course, I realize that daring to declare God's truth could come across as yet more evidence of arrogance on my part—actually, though, it is meant as an admission of my inability and insignificance. I would never hazard on the merits of my own ideas or thoughts to tell you definitively anything about even the most trivial part of the most inconsequential aspect of your life . . . well, actually, that's probably not true. Sinful man that I am, it's not inconceivable that given the chance, I might pontificate all sorts of opinions about stuff that is none of my business. In this book, though, I will resist the temptation to spout opinion or offer my own ideas—as insightful and important as I think those may be. No, what I write is what I have been given to write. It's been given to me by the church, which ordained me as a pastor and called me as a teacher. I will write circumspectly and carefully, but without academic evasion and equivocation. And hopefully, if I am successful, without academic posturing and obscurity. I will strive, as faithfully as I can, to tell you God's truth about your life.

I already noted that this is not a book about your body, per se. I'm not a physician or a biologist. This is definitely not a book about the intricate and amazing workings of your body. I'll leave that important work to others. Of course, issues related to our lives within the purview of what might be called the hard sciences do tell us vitally important things about ourselves. But they are inherently limited only to problems and subjects that can be measured, calculated, and replicated. The transfer of DNA from one cell to another, the ideal oxygenation of blood, or the best food to eat for building muscle are ably handled by the appropriate expert in each particular field. But if what we know about life is limited only to what we can observe, measure, quantify, and manage, we won't know much about the things that matter most.

Put in terms that would have been familiar to the ancients—well, actually to anyone living before the seventeenth-century rise of what is called modernity and the science that goes with it—we can learn about the material aspects of our lives (the material cause) and even the interactions and influences that shape our lives (the instrumental cause) from the work of science; but science can only detect a portion of the plans and forms that constitute our lives (the formal cause) and will never be able to discern the goal or reason for our lives (the final cause).[1] Coming to terms with one's place in the world is a project that cannot be trusted to science—that route can end only in desperate meaninglessness, will-to-power bravado, or

1 Aristotle's idea of the four causes, or explanations, remains an exceedingly useful method for thinking about and understanding a thing or event. His ancient sort of taxonomy forces every honest thinker to acknowledge the glaring limits of all science in both its hard and soft forms. Regardless the amount of truth gained by modern man in the realm of material and efficient causes, the remaining questions of a thing's formal and final causes resist or completely defy measurement and naturalistic explanation.

sentimental silliness. And offering a definitive account of the final reason for one's life, or the ultimate aim of what it's all about, is a project that necessarily confounds all science. These are questions that belong to philosophers—or better yet, to theologians. These are the questions that interest me and that occupy this book. And the best and only trustworthy answers to these questions, I am convinced, can have but one source: the One who designed and made the world.

This truth has been expressed capably by many people, and not a few of them have suggested some form of what can be called the cake metaphor. Give a group of researchers a three-tier cake and they can tell you definitively about its color, size, weight, age, caloric content, and physical composition. They could even perhaps offer some conjectures on its place in the world based on some of those observable factors—any lettering or decoration or presence of artificial preservatives, for example, could provide clues about where, when, and by whom it might have been made. And they might have some thoughts to offer about the artistic or possible sentimental meaning of the cake. But the final purpose of that cake, its goal or end (the classic Greek term is *telos*) and therefore also its ultimate *meaning* in the universe, could be rightly discerned only by consulting and understanding those who had baked or perhaps bought the cake and so determined its final purpose. Was the cake's reason for existence to celebrate a birthday, send off a retiring coworker, provide an energy boost to a sports team, or simply to meet a corporate quota for chocolate cake production only to be tossed into a dumpster after sitting too long on a shelf and being shunned even in the supermarket's discounted section? Only the one who creates and controls the cake knows for sure.

The same basic truth holds even in the case of a far more complex thing like a human life. What is that life's purpose and meaning? Only the One who creates and controls that life knows for sure (which, incidentally, mercifully disqualifies us from that task). If the Creator and Lord is not consulted, then every effort to discern the final cause or even the full picture of the formal cause of a human life is doomed to fail—even if that failure is not immediately recognized. This truth is all the more valid when it is the human person himself who defies reality and undertakes the task of determining the meaning and purpose of his own life. No person is his own creator, and so no person is equipped to determine his own telos. Notwithstanding the prevailing wisdom of the whole of our modern or even, if you are so persuaded, postmodern Western culture, the crucial question of the meaning of a person's own life is not up to each person to decide.

A THEOLOGICAL ANSWER

My purpose in this book is quite simple, then. As one called to the task of theology, I will tackle the questions that touch on the formal and the final causes of your life—the fundamental relationships, responsibilities, and purposes that shape your life along with the ultimate goal or fulfillment that rightly aims your life. As overambitious as this may sound, it is actually fully and safely within the parameters of theology, because these are questions that can be answered only by the Creator, who is, of course, by definition the author, director, and subject of all faithful theology. I will provide answers that are firmly grounded in and normed by the teaching of the Christian church. Naturally, all that I think, and so all that I write, is always colored by my own particular place within Christianity that is called Lutheranism. But just as that tradition, when practiced faithfully, seeks only to be in the center of the received teachings of the church, so will I strive to provide answers to life's biggest questions in ways that are solidly in the central stream of the flow of Christian doctrine.

Using the rubric of the formal cause can shed perhaps a bit more light on the reason for this book and so better equip you for what lies ahead. Besides the obvious influences of the church and the academy, which have formed me from the day I was born, the most direct impetus behind this book is twofold. First, there is my own observation of the utter emptiness and futility that lies at the center of so many lives in the world today. A world drained of universal truth and realities that hold inviolable for all people in all places is a world that also loses the ability to suggest a meaning or purpose in life beyond what each person can devise for himself. For the vast majority of people, this becomes little more than seeking to enhance the "amplitude in living itself," as the prescient and pessimistic American sociologist Philip Rieff once declared.[2] It's the idea put less eloquently but more bluntly and perhaps memorably in the Schlitz commercials of my youth: "You only go around once, you gotta grab for all the gusto you can." Making life more meaningful by filling it with things that make it bigger and better is the modern solution to the problem of a meaningless life. Sadly, the pursuit of this elusive and false goal proves so engrossing and temporarily satisfying that vast swaths of humanity fail to realize the futility and folly of living so trivially and pointlessly until years of time and resources have already been wasted. Yet more sadly and tragically, far too many reach the end of life still trying to determine the point of it all. Going for gusto may sell beer and even drive the world's economic engine, but it will not bring meaning to life. This book aims to address that sad tragedy by presenting a clear and explicit answer to the meaning of life—yes, your life.

2 Philip Rieff, *The Triumph of the Therapeutic: Uses of Faith after Freud* (Chicago: University of Chicago Press, 1966), 22.

The other, more immediate force behind this book is an evolving graduate course I've taught several times now called "Work & Art." In this case, which as every college student knows is not always the case, the class is about exactly what the title says. Surprisingly enough, the topic of work is actually worthy of rather extensive and thoughtful study, not only in the realms of history, economics, and sociology, but also theology. While some aspect of work figures prominently in the lives of every single person, it is rather remarkable that most people expend little effort and pay almost no attention to what they actually think and understand about the very idea of work. Is it merely a means to an end—the requisite capital for a life filled with pursuing gusto; or is it the basis for the defining purpose and meaning of life—exemplified by the laborer who can, with glowing satisfaction and even joy, declare at the end of a workday, "I was born to do this!"?

But what happens to work if the meaning of life is something other than the mere amplification of lifestyle and pleasure or even the work itself? Indeed, if, as some will argue, life is not about work at all but is only rightly centered on the quiet contemplation of the truths of the universe and the delight of being alive in the creation, then where does work fit, if at all? And what if your work is demeaning and degrading or soul-crushing and so, as Marx would famously put it, alienating to your very humanity? When does work stop and play begin? Can a life of contemplation be reconciled with a life of activity? Is it really just a matter of balance—a very old truth that is endlessly repackaged in new ways to sell more books? These are the sort of questions that overflow in a class on work and art. Having picked my way through this heap of ideas for several years, I am ready now to weigh in with an answer that I'm convinced is thoroughly grounded in Christian doctrine and so is true.

In the chapters that follow, I will explore work and its place in our lives, along with the relationship of work to the purpose and telos of every human life. But this is not a book only about work and art and rest and play. More importantly, and more comprehensively, this is a book about the meaning of life and the place of each human within God's remarkable masterpiece called creation—the divine work that surrounds and enfolds every human life. There is a great deal to be said in favor of seeing the purpose of life as a contemplation or, perhaps better, a savoring of the wonders of the Creator and his creation and the relationships and connections that bind it all together as the Master Creator designed it. The ancients, and for generations also the church, called this sort of reflection *leisure*, which will likely and rightly sound strange in many ears but will be more fully explained in the pages that follow. In this book, then, I will address the question of the interrelationship of a life of contemplation over against a life of activity and also offer a few thoughts about the place of art and beauty within the driving question of the point of life—your life.

To do this job well, I will need to delve a bit into a topic I have learned to see with new eyes and ever-growing appreciation as it defines and shapes the lives we live and comprehends and enhances all that has been mentioned in this introduction in ways that may very well surprise a few readers. I am convinced that there is more to the Decalogue's commandment enjoining us, "Remember the Sabbath day," than most Christians have learned to see and appreciate. This is a foundational and, I am convinced, biblical idea that deserves careful attention. As it is used in the Bible, *sabbath* names and shapes the ultimate purpose and objective of creation and human life in ways that are profound and far-reaching. Exploring with some care our understanding of sabbath and its essential and continuing importance for our lives will occupy our attention in the first chapters. With that foundation in place, I'll pick up the questions about work and leisure and the meaning of our lives.

My goal, my telos, for this book, is to write with a candor and clarity that simply spells out what I believe to be true about your life. I have no doubt that there will be some, perhaps many, who will disagree with parts or even much of the argument I present; but I will make my case and will do it in a way that seeks always both to be normed by the church's teaching and presented in a way that makes sense to you, my reader. You are, after all, the immediate final cause for this book—or at least one of them (in truth, I have a multitude of reasons for writing). Still, a driving and animating goal for this book that was continually in the forefront of my thinking as I wrote is to make a difference for you. My goal is to help you come to terms with what it means to be a human in your particular time and place, to help you figure out the point of it all, and to help you discover the wonderful meaning and fullness of your life as God intended it, a meaning that can fill, enhance, and transform every minute of every day of your entire life. Yes, this book's aim is nothing less than telling you about the meaning, purpose, and goal of your life. The words and the voice are mine, of course, but the truth is from God.

...r reason for
live the
...wn & Out Life.

Delighting in the Down a...
Out Life

Day 7: Embracing God's
Sabbath and Gi...
work, rest, or pla...
Re-thinking Sabb...

Joy fully living
Down and Out
Life and the Joy
Brings

Sabbath and the M...
of Existence

The Point of it All

Gift + Plan
Design for the
Down and Out
Life

Your Reason for B...

Sabbath Work: Re-Thinking ...
Rest

God's Plan for

Receiving God...

CHAPTER 1

SABBATH IN THE CATECHISM

LEARNING THE COMMANDMENT

The exact time and place are no longer clear, but I assume it was in one of the classrooms created by closing the now retro-cool, mid-century bifold doors in the fellowship hall of Our Savior Lutheran Church in Gladwin, Michigan. It was there that I was catechized by my father and pastor (effectively collapsing all distinction between home and church). It was there that I first gave thought to the Third Commandment and its meaning. Of course, in Lutheran circles, the *meaning* of any given commandment indicates much more than unspecified run-of-the mill interpretations or the insights of thoughtful readers searching for the significance of a text. No, for Lutherans a commandment's (or article's or petition's) *meaning* is a technical term for the official answer to *the* catechism question: "What does this mean?" (which can't help but sound far more compelling in the rhythm of the original German: "*Was ist das?*"). The answer to each successive question in our textbook, the Small Catechism, was supplied, of course, by Martin Luther. What I learned in confirmation class is that the Third Commandment, "Remember the Sabbath day to keep it holy," means, "We should fear and love God that we may not despise preaching and His Word, but hold it sacred and gladly hear and learn it." Given my age, of course I learned this from the "old blue" version of Luther's Small Catechism,[1] which, it turns out, is almost exactly the way it still appears in the latest version of the CPH catechism; though the latest edition inconsequentially replaces "to keep" with "by keeping" and swaps "may not despise" with "do not despise," the meaning is the same.[2] My own preconfirmation

1 *A Short Explanation of Dr. Martin Luther's Small Catechism: A Handbook of Christian Doctrine* (St. Louis: Concordia Publishing House, 1943).

2 *Luther's Small Catechism with Explanation* (St. Louis: Concordia Publishing House, 2017).

catechesis was decades ago, but I still remember being struck even then by the oddity of Luther's explanation of the Third Commandment.

When Luther unpacked the meaning of all the other commandments, he fleshed them out into robust applications that were sweeping, far-reaching, and impossibly demanding for a twelve-year-old—or for a sixty-two-year-old, for that matter. The Fifth Commandment, for example, doesn't just mean don't murder anyone, but it means that we can't even harbor ill feelings of hatred for any human being, and even more, we need to do whatever we can to help our neighbors in any and every bodily need. That was and is a rather mind-boggling, overwhelming expectation, which I learned, of course, is precisely the point. Who can do such a thing? No one—well, no one but Jesus. At least that's how I came to understand the Lutheran emphasis on the accusing use or function of the law; but that's another topic for another time.[3] The inexplicable thing about the Third Commandment is that Luther seemed to move in the exact opposite direction; instead of infinitely and impossibly expanding the commandment's import, he narrowed and contracted it. He even seemed to redirect it, ignoring entirely the prohibition against work. For Luther, keeping the sabbath basically means going to church and paying attention—at least, that's the boiled-down version that came through to me in my youth. This was welcome news to a junior high boy for whom faithful Sunday church attendance was never in question; if there was a service, I was there. The Third Commandment was a virtual gimme. Just as long as I didn't allow my mind to wander into too much daydreaming during the sermon, I was golden. The Third Commandment, then, didn't align with

3 Those interested in that topic, the uses or functions of the law in the life of a believer and the old and continuing Lutheran struggle over the number and importance of those uses, can consult my book *A Case for Character* (Minneapolis: Fortress, 2014).

the rest. Every other commandment's meaning was grounded directly in the specific direction from the Decalogue and grew fat and demanding as Luther unpacked and amplified what it meant. But not the Third Commandment. That one was cut and dried. To keep the sabbath, I just had to go to church, pay attention, and perhaps—a bit more piously—read my Bible with some regularity. This thin take on the meaning of the commandment struck even the young and exceedingly ignorant boy that I then was as a tad truncated and narrow. But who was I to question what was in the catechism—and who was I to argue with Luther?

Indeed, it is rarely a good idea to argue with Luther; I know that truth exceedingly well. It is truer for me now than it was then. Still, I suspect that my experience of being a trifle perplexed by the singular nature of Luther's atypically restrictive handling of the Third Commandment is not entirely unique to me. It may come as a surprise to those who bear the great reformer's name, but when it comes to the sabbath commandment, Lutherans stand out in Christendom with the notoriety of an exceptionally idiosyncratic and simple view. While other Christians fret interminably about the extent to which the sabbath has been set aside in the New Testament, how much work they may do or not do and what actually constitutes work on the sabbath, and even about what day exactly is the sabbath that must be kept with some restrictions on work, Lutherans are apparently able to vanquish all the demanding rigor of the sabbath commandment merely by going to church—or maybe even by just tuning in or logging on to a reliably good sermon source. Having dispensed with that duty, they are good to go, free to use the remaining 23+ hours of any given Sunday any way that they choose.[4] From what I have observed among the members of

4 Those interested in learning more about typical Christian, that is, Protestant, debates about sabbath-keeping can check out Christopher John Donato, ed., *Perspectives on the Sabbath: Four Views* (Nashville: B&H Publishing Group, 2011).

my synod, my portrayal is only slightly exaggerated if at all. For Lutherans, keeping the sabbath means honoring God's Word by going to church, and that covers it.

So, what accounts for the marked contrast between the Lutheran approach to the Third Commandment and the rest of the church that is usually quite interested in exploring and establishing careful guidelines for what can and cannot be done on a Sunday (or a Saturday) in order to keep the sabbath commandment rightly? Why does this commandment receive such an attenuated interpretation by Luther? While the details of the story would require far more historical and doctrinal exposition than this present volume allows or needs, the heart of the answer lies—as it so often does—in the immediate social and ecclesiastical context that shaped Luther's world. Luther was not the only reformer, of course, and his were not the only ideas swirling through European parishes in the early sixteenth century. Some of those catching the spirit of reformation were eager to take the movement in directions for which Luther had no stomach at all. Of course, it is well known that Luther directed his efforts at reforming the church against the errors of Rome, but it needs to be remembered that he contended with equal zeal against the errors of other reformers. Both sides, as he saw it, were too often guilty of subverting the truth of the gospel as revealed in Christ, detailed in Scripture, and taught by faithful churchmen. His erstwhile follower and reformation supporter Andreas Karlstadt serves as a ready and relevant example of Luther's dealings with those who fell into the camp of excessive and errant reform.[5]

5 Often these reformers are lumped together under the heading of "The Radical Reformation" as opposed to the magisterial reformers like Luther and Calvin, but it should be kept in mind that there is a wide diversity of teaching among those under either label.

THE PROBLEM OF KARLSTADT

It was Karlstadt who had been left to mind things in Wittenberg while Luther was "kidnapped" for safekeeping at the Wartburg following his line-in-the-sand appearance at the Diet of Worms. But Karlstadt failed to serve as a faithful steward diligently preserving the new status quo while waiting for the return of Luther. Karlstadt was eager to serve as the champion of a thoroughgoing anti-Roman cleansing of the church. He pushed for further, more aggressive, and, in Luther's estimation, unnecessarily disruptive and thus errant reforms. Among other things, Karlstadt summarily dispensed with all clerical vestments, was joined in marriage to a fifteen-year-old girl, oversaw the purging of all images from church buildings, and urged that true Christians should adhere to the law of Moses—in particular, the laws relating to sabbath and the prohibition of work. Karlstadt was a busy man, accomplishing all of this in a mere handful of months over the winter of 1521–22. But when spring came, so did Luther. The fugitive in hiding cut short his Wartburg exile precisely because of the situation in Wittenberg. As soon as he arrived home, Luther got to work doing his best to straighten out the mess made by his one-time disciple. The bigger problem was that Karlstadt was not simply a shocking anomaly. He was one of many who were suggesting things that, at the time, were completely radical. Some of the suggestions have since become commonplace in the church, while others remain every bit as outlandish now as they were then. It was the last-mentioned of Karlstadt's over-the-top reforms that is most relevant for my present concern: his advocacy for a Jewish-style keeping of the sabbath.

To be sure, Karlstadt's own position on the sabbath allowed for some nuance and wasn't as legalistic as the image we have of Pharisees unwilling to lift a finger or orthodox Jews searching out Gentile goyim willing to light their ovens on the sabbath.[6] Still, his bottom line was that to obey the Third Commandment, one needed to refrain from doing any sort of work. That was the recurrent central theme of his teaching on the matter: "God forbade human beings to work on the sabbath. And everything we, our children, and our cattle might do, God has canceled; everything is to be at rest on the day on which we pray God for holiness."[7] But not only did Karlstadt center his understanding of the sabbath on the prohibition of work, he took things even further, viewing the day through a decidedly dour lens, intent to drain from the sabbath any semblance of joy and instead to multiply the burden and misery of the day. Karlstadt made his point explicitly: "Someone might now ask what a person is to do on the sabbath to pass the long time or [overcome] boredom. Answer: We ought to be idle, do nothing, and endure the long time. The sabbath has been instituted for the spirit to reach a point of boredom and learn something during the idle time."[8] Presumably, the lesson Karlstadt hoped was learned was the need for grace that would manifest itself in a prayer for holiness. For Karlstadt, every sabbath was a tedious, austere day for sober and weary self-reflection.

As far as Luther was concerned, this "Sabbatarian" understanding of the commandment erred badly in a number of ways. It was wrong to revivify a law intended, as he saw it, only for the Jewish nation and to make it a law imposed on every Christian. Luther spelled this out pointedly in his essay "How Christians Should Regard Moses." His position is sweeping: "For Paul

6 To read what Karlstadt actually taught, see "Regarding the Sabbath and Statutory Holy Days (1524)" in E. J. Furcha, ed., *The Essential Carlstadt: Fifteen Tracts by Andreas Bodenstein (Carlstadt) from Karlstadt* (Waterloo, Ontario: Herald Press, 1995), 317–38.

7 Ibid., 333.

8 Ibid., 332–33.

and the New Testament abolish the sabbath, to show us that the sabbath was given to the Jews alone, for whom it is a stern commandment."[9] Luther rightly understood that Karlstadt's emphasis disastrously put Moses in the spotlight instead of Christ, gutted the new freedom inaugurated by the work of Christ (and spelled out in the first church council as related in Acts 15), and introduced a legalism antithetical to the very nature of Christian confession. In short, Luther wanted nothing to do with the Sabbatarian way of doing things. This reprised legalism was a move away from Christ and his gospel and in the direction of Moses and his law. It relinquished all that Luther had only recently discovered and made known to the church about the free gift of grace, captured in the central Lutheran teaching of justification.[10]

This, I believe, is the critical thing to understand when considering what Luther says and doesn't say about the meaning of the Third Commandment in his Small Catechism. Luther understood that, seen from this side of Jesus' resurrection, the Third Commandment cannot possibly be about refusing to do any work on a Sunday (or a Saturday if you happen to be a stickler for the seventh day). Instead, the heart of the commandment, its essence for Christians, is the need to be where God's gifts are delivered and to be present when the grace is bestowed in the preached Word. Understanding this context readily accounts for the simplicity and limited nature of, not to mention the complete absence of any mention of work or rest in, Luther's interpretation of the commandment in the Small Catechism.

9 Martin Luther, *Luther's Works,* vol. 35, *Word and Sacrament*, ed. E. Theodore Bachmann (Philadelphia: Fortress Press, 1960), 165. Used by permission of Augsburg Publishing House.

10 This is, of course, articulated succinctly and confessionally by Melanchthon in the Augsburg Confession, Article IV, which declares in no uncertain terms that we are justified by grace through faith in Jesus Christ alone.

Naturally, there is more to the story than merely Luther's unmitigated doctrinal rejection of Karlstadt's attempt at hyper-reform, more even than the degree of personal regret or frustration Luther may have harbored toward his old colleague now turned adversary. Relevant to Luther's focused interpretation of the Third Commandment, and his interpretation of all the commandments, were also questions about

- what it meant for Christ to have fulfilled the law;
- the distinctions, often sought and rarely fully solved, between the moral law, the ceremonial law, and the political law of Israel;
- the way that Christian freedom interfaced with vocational responsibilities toward other creatures;
- the relation of the Decalogue to the natural law.

These issues were all in the air as Luther penned his elegant and timeless answers in his Small Catechism to the repeated question "*Was ist das?*" Many of those same bullet-point issues are relevant for us yet today and still capable of fueling lively discussions among believers. I will address them to the extent necessary, especially the last point, as I work to unpack the meaning of sabbath for twenty-first-century Christians as we move along in the next chapter.[11] For now, for the sake of fairness to Luther, it is sufficient to probe just a bit more into his understanding of what it meant to keep the sabbath. I began the chapter by noting Luther's terse treatment of the sabbath commandment in the Small Catechism. Quite fittingly, he explores

11 For those interested in probing these matters further and more deeply than I will be doing, especially the structure of the Commandments flowing out of the First Commandment and the Christological lens at work in Luther's reading of the Commandments, an excellent presentation can be found in *Perspectives on the Sabbath*, ed. Donato. My colleague Charles Arand ably and accurately provided the Lutheran perspective.

and explains his thinking more fully in the Large Catechism.

Compared to the Small Catechism, the Large Catechism is certainly longer, but it is still far from verbose. Luther spends a scant four pages of his larger catechism explaining the meaning of the Third Commandment. He employs his usual approach: account for the plain meaning of the text and then set forth its application to Christians today. He understands the commandment, "You are to hallow the day of rest," as he cited it from his own translation, in the first place as a directive "given to the Jews alone. They were to refrain from hard work and to rest, so that both human beings and animals might be refreshed and not be exhausted by constant labor."[12] Given its narrow cultural and historical application, Luther declared, "This commandment does not concern us Christians."[13] In other words, since this was a commandment only for the people of Israel, it is no longer required of Christians to refrain from doing work on the seventh day.

THE DEEPER MEANING

The fact that Luther actually offered some commentary and teaching on the commandment shows, however, that Luther did think that there was more to the commandment than the mere "outward meaning" aimed at the ancient people of Israel and the specific rules they were to follow in their particular situation. The Third Commandment also reflected, as did all the commandments, truths about the natural law—God's will for his creation, hardwired into the very fabric of the world and his creatures. Considered from this perspective, Luther suggested that the commandment meant two things: people who work hard as God directed them to work need a chance to rest, and setting aside one day in seven accomplished this; and given a

12 Large Catechism, Ten Commandments, paragraph 80.

13 Ibid., paragraph 82.

day without work, people would be free to attend worship and "hear and discuss God's Word and then to offer praise, song, and prayer to God."[14] This, of course, brings us back to the Word-and-worship-focused explanation of the Small Catechism.

Tracing Luther's logic helps make sense of why his Small Catechism understanding of keeping the sabbath can boil down to going to church and paying attention. While the command to stop work applies only to Israel, the obligation to hallow the day of rest applies to all people for all time—that is, it is part of the natural law. So how does one hallow the day? Allowing tired bodies a day to rest each week is important, no doubt; Luther grants this without becoming at all concerned about on which day this happens. What concerns Luther is making a day holy by honoring God in all of life and so making all the things and days in one's life holy. Luther fully understands, however, that the work of making holy is never accomplished by the actions or attitudes of people. Consistent with the heart of his teaching, Luther knew that holiness comes not by human work but only by the work of God. "Accordingly," Luther wrote, "I constantly repeat that all our life and work must be based on God's Word if they are to be God-pleasing or holy."[15] Put another way, it is not our doing or not doing that makes a task, person, or day holy. It is always and only God through his work on our behalf who makes things holy. And, of course, God accomplishes this work through his Word—his promised and standard way of being present and working in the world. And further, of course, that active, sanctifying Word is heard where it is preached. The progression is complete and consistent. One hallows the sabbath, not by refusing to work or by cultivating idle boredom or even by ginning up a morose melancholy repentance, but by attending to the sanctifying Word of God, which makes holy

14 Ibid., paragraph 84.

15 Ibid., paragraph 92.

all who hear it and follow it. "Remember, then, that you must be concerned not only about hearing the Word, but also about learning it and retaining it. . . . It is the commandment of God, who will require of you an accounting of how you have heard, learned, and honored his Word."[16]

So, Luther does not ignore the rest component of the sabbath. He knows the Old Testament specifically tied resting from all work with the keeping of the sabbath.[17] But based on the New Testament's handling of sabbath and his understanding of the relation between natural law and specific applications of the law in a particular time and place, typically known as positive law, he concludes that this prohibition of work is culture-specific and so dismisses that particular aspect while seeking to retain what he believes is the eternal, moral directive foundationally underlying the specific command aimed at Israel. A couple contemporary examples might help shed some light on this procedure. Drivers on US interstates are ordinarily forbidden to exceed seventy miles per hour (unless driving in some parts of the high plains, where those so inclined are generously permitted to cruise at eighty). This statute, an instance of positive law, has meaning for us in the twenty-first century, but none for people living only one hundred years ago—or perhaps for people living one hundred years in the future. The foundational truth on which the current law is based, however, has been and will always be in force in this world: don't jeopardize another's life or well-being by your own reckless behavior. Similarly, there are complex laws against insider trading that hold meaning only for a handful of those who operate in the rarified realms of high finance. But the principle of not taking what is not yours whether by force or by cheating holds for all time and in all places.

16 Ibid., paragraph 98.

17 See Exodus 31:15; 35:2; Leviticus 23:3; Deuteronomy 5:14.

When it comes to the Third Commandment, then, Luther concludes that the specific prohibition against working on the seventh day is the external, culture-specific manifestation of a foundational idea. And in this case, as he presents his thinking in the Large Catechism, it seems that Luther recognizes two prongs of timeless natural law truth that undergird the sabbath commandment. One is simply the rather obvious, common-sense need for created beings to be given a chance to rest from their labor, and the other is the even more profound emphasis on God's activity in his Word as the only means by which created beings and the time they inhabit can be made holy. It is, of course, the latter that drives his interpretation of the commandment in the Small Catechism.

CATECHETICAL HISTORY

With an adequate understanding of Luther's treatment of the Third Commandment in place, it is time now to leap forward several centuries and consider the way that recent catechisms produced by Concordia Publishing House (CPH) handle the sabbath commandment. But before diving into that task, a brief word of explanation and a personal confession of sorts are in order. Luther's Small Catechism is actually quite small. And while this may seem rather a tautological statement, it came as quite a surprise to me when I finally realized it—and that at a much later date than I am eager to admit. Toting our navy blue catechisms to Wednesday afternoon confirmation class was hardly a chore for my eighth-grade classmates and me. The book was literally little.[18] So, the title seemed quite appropriate; it was indeed *Luther's Small Catechism*.

18 For those fond of details, it measured 5 × 7½ inches and was just over 5/8 of an inch thick with 221 pages tightly bound between the hard covers. By contrast, the newest version measures 5¼ × 8¼ and is 1¼ inches thick with 429 pages.

In retrospect, maybe I can assuage some of the embarrassment of my older self by pointing out that nowhere on the cover or on the title page of that volume was there any indication that anyone other than Luther himself was involved in writing the entire contents of my eighth-grade catechism. Quite likely, my mind was otherwise occupied (and my mouth otherwise engaged) when the data point that Luther did not in fact write the bulk of our catechism was shared with the class—for some students, memorizing all six chief parts with their meanings was far easier than learning appropriate classroom behavior. When, much later in life, it finally dawned on me that the vast majority of the questions and answers in the "Small Catechism" that had served as my doctrinal textbook in preparation for confirmation was actually written by a committee under the supervision of the synodical president, I was dumbfounded and not a little humbled. A happy consequence is that I've since tried to cultivate a genuine sympathy for students preparing for pastoral ministry who seem with remarkable regularity to be caught completely unawares by some disconcerting doctrinal surprise or another that rattles their settled world. In my case, I was stunned to realize that Luther had only written the first 35 of the 221 pages in my *Luther's Small Catechism*, while all the rest of the careful doctrinal teaching presented in the form of questions and answers came from a myriad of authors spread across many years. Later editions of catechisms from CPH now add "with Explanation" on the cover. Perhaps that means that learners of later generations have been spared the confusion I experienced. Nevertheless, I've developed the habit, whenever I teach anything from the Small Catechism, of stressing the difference between the Small Catechism that Luther wrote and the additional two or three or four hundred pages of text subsequently supplied by assorted theologians in the church. Interestingly enough, this also helps explain how "Luther's Catechism" can deal with questions about Mormons, Jehovah's Witnesses, same-sex marriage, and Wicca—a fact I used to chalk up to modern tweaks!

What all this means, then, is that the shape and content of the doctrinal questions and answers that serve as the authoritative theological textbook for an entire synod are altogether dependent on those who write, edit, and review them. And the catechisms published by CPH matter a great deal because they have made and continue to make a profound impact on the doctrinal content and understanding of millions of Lutherans. In other words, the way that any particular synodical version of Luther's Small Catechism goes about explaining the text of Luther's Small Catechism is exceedingly important for the way that believers understand the Christian faith. All of this is especially relevant for the way the Third Commandment is explained and taught.

What is interesting, and what perhaps accounts for my original perplexity when encountering Luther's Third Commandment in my youth, is that the expanded explanation of the commandment in the "little blue" catechism that comprised my preconfirmation catechesis mentions none of the wider material Luther explores in the Large Catechism. The message in the 1943 catechism, the one I carried to catechism class, was unequivocal. The very first question and answer, Question 45, said it all:

> Does God require that we Christians of the New Testament observe the Sabbath (Saturday) and other holy days of the Old Testament?
>
> *He does not;* for in the New Testament the Sabbath

> and other holy days were *abolished by God Himself.*[19]

After this summary dismissal, the 1943 explanation moves directly into stern instruction about the importance of going to church and reading God's Word. The Synod's 1991 update of *Luther's Small Catechism with Explanation* (the "bright blue one" that later became the "maroon one") softened the dismissive tone somewhat. Answering the query whether "God requires us to observe the Sabbath and other holy days of the Old Testament," it teaches: "The Sabbath was a sign pointing to Jesus, who is our rest. Since Jesus has come as our Savior and Lord, God no longer requires us to observe the Sabbath day and other holy days of the Old Testament."[20] From there it followed the path of its predecessor and turned its full attention exclusively to questions related to worship and Bible reading with the same final admonition: "We should diligently spread the Word."[21] All of this is consistent with Luther's Small Catechism focus.

So, is Luther's narrow focus the right approach? Taking into account the absolute necessity that God's Word must be at work for any aspect of holiness to be possible, it is obvious that Luther's move is on target. And considering his immediate context, his limited application of the commandment also makes sense. But is it sufficient? Does it do justice to the intent of the commandment? Is it enough to limit the Third Commandment to a call to be attentive to God's Word? Is this tight reading of the commandment even consistent with Luther's own way of operating with all the other nine commandments? The answer

19 *A Short Explanation of Dr. Martin Luther's Small Catechism.* Italics in original.

20 *Luther's Small Catechism with Explanation* (St. Louis: Concordia Publishing House, 1991), Question 36.

21 Ibid., Question 40D.

to the last question is actually easy to answer. It is clearly no. While the other nine commandments are interpreted by the reformer in ways that make them wide, sweeping, and increasingly expansive in scope, Luther's approach to the Third Commandment does the opposite. While we can understand and appreciate his reasons for doing this and affirm the clear focus on the centrality of God's Word for any sabbath-keeping—and frankly for any real keeping of any of the Commandments—perhaps it is not too audacious to wonder nevertheless if there might be even more to the commandment. Maybe there is something foundational and expansive going on behind and underneath the ancient command to Israel to refrain from doing any work on the seventh day that surpasses even the need to establish times for attending to God's enlivening Word. Perhaps there is more to consider as we "remember the Sabbath day, to keep it holy."[22]

Of course, we have yet to mention one more edition of *Luther's Small Catechism with Explanation*—that book intended to serve as the foundation for the basic catechesis of the whole church and especially her youth. After a long and thorough updating, the most recent iteration of the Small Catechism appeared in 2017, smartly dressed in black with a maroon spine.[23] Like its twentieth-century predecessors, the focus of the most recent edition is again on worship and attention to God's Word. It even includes a new question and corresponding answer about the value of liturgical worship, complete with a point-by-point overview of the basic elements of the Divine Service.[24] But before it jumps into the necessary work

22 Exodus 20:8. Unless otherwise noted, Scripture quotations are from the 1995 NASB translation.

23 *Luther's Small Catechism with Explanation* (St. Louis: Concordia Publishing House, 2017).

24 Ibid., Question 53.

of explaining Luther's Word-oriented explanation, this edition hints at something more.

A standard and welcome feature new to the 2017 edition's format is a short section titled "The Central Thought," which appears immediately after each of Luther's explanations and then is followed with the familiar, expanded question-and-answer discussion under the guiding headings "A Closer Reading of the Small Catechism" and "Connections and Applications." In the case of the Third Commandment, we are told "The Central Thought" is that "God invites us to rest, reflect on His Word, and receive His forgiveness in order to strengthen our faith in Him." Then, setting the stage for what is to come and perhaps fomenting some thinking or even discussion, readers are asked, "When people today set aside time for rest, how do they spend that time?" They are directed to read the story of Mary and Martha and then open-endedly asked, "Why does Jesus commend Mary and not hardworking Martha?"[25] It seems as if everything has been prepared for a leap into the attentive hearing of God's Word and the Divine Service, where this happens week after week.

Before starting down that well-worn track, though, we read this remarkable sentence, highlighted by an ornate red cross bullet point and printed in boldface: "As Christians, God's Word leads us to delight in His wondrous works of creation and redemption." Immediately after this potent but seemingly unrelated observation, we are prompted with another question without a given answer, "How does God's Word open our eyes to see all of His good works?"[26] The significance of this poignant addition encouraging wonder and delight grounded in creation and redemption becomes more apparent when we observe that this idea is presented as a basic and independent reality and

25 Ibid., p. 74.
26 Ibid.

no direct connection to the discussion of faithful church attendance that follows is offered. This addition to the discussion is both significant and exactly right. It suggests an understanding of the Third Commandment's application to our lives today that is wonderfully robust, is endlessly interesting, and entails far more than merely cultivating a habit of faithful church attendance. This thought will take shape much more fully in the pages to come.

The first of the questions that discuss the commandment and Luther's explanation, Question 48, continues this fresh expansion by asking, "What is the Sabbath day?" and then answering its own question: "In the Old Testament, God set aside the seventh day (Saturday) as a day of rest for His people to worship and to ponder A. the power and goodness of God in His work of creation; B. the graciousness of God's work of redemption." As we will see later, and as noted with the Bible verses supplied after each part of the answer, these points reflect the pair of reasons offered in the Bible for the keeping of the sabbath.[27] The first reason maps to God's work of creation and seventh-day rest, and the second to God's work of liberation in the exodus.

Question 49 then keys into the rest and worship aspects of the ancient command when it responds to its own question, "What were some features of the Sabbath in the Old Testament?" with "A. The Sabbath provided time for physical rest. B. The Sabbath provided time for spiritual rest through worship, fellowship, and devotion to God's Word and promises."[28] This direction faithfully follows Luther's lead in the Large Catechism, where he emphasizes the foundational ideas of the need for physical rest for weary souls coupled with the need for spiritual

27 The two vital passages quoted are Exodus 20:8–11 and Deuteronomy 5:12, 15.

28 *Luther's Small Catechism with Explanation* (2017).

renewal for depleted and sinful souls delivered through hearing God's Word. But one final note at the end of Question 49 drops a further word that is not immediately concerned with hearing God's Word and is wonderfully pregnant with possibilities as it states: "Rest was part of the rhythm that God put in place for His Old Testament Church."[29] Indeed in creation itself, in resting from his own work on the seventh day, God established the rhythm that would guide and shape the lives of the human creatures made in his image. As the 2017 catechism observes, for Israel this was codified in commands to give people and animals a day of rest after six days of work, to give the land a year of rest after six years of harvest, and to erase debts after seven sets of seven years during the fiftieth year of jubilee. The key reality at work under all these particular commands is the power of the sabbath rhythm itself that establishes God's intentions for his creation.

These motions in the 2017 catechism in the direction of creation, redemption, and the rhythm of work and sabbath built into the very fabric of the creation by the action and example of the Creator himself are tantalizing, but they are also as far as this newest version of the Small Catechism takes the thought. It is a pity that this suggestive direction was not pursued further. But it would also be naïvely ignorant of the church's metabolism and behavior to expect so wholesale a change in the space of a single revision of our lodestar book of instruction. That some vitally critical ideas for understanding sabbath—like creation, rhythm, and rest—have finally made an appearance in the core textbook of The Lutheran Church—Missouri Synod (LCMS) should not go unnoticed or unappreciated. And with such a beginning, perhaps there is more reason to be hopeful about what might be accomplished in subsequent editions—there is certainly a rich palette of colors still available that might be used

29 Ibid.

for the cover (just a thought, but a shade of green might be nice when the time comes).

SITUATING THE SABBATH

There are no further versions of the catechism left to explore, which is likely a welcome word of consolation for my reader whose patience has already been tried by the tedium of this chapter. There remains, though, one obvious question demanding an answer: "What's the point of all this meticulous digging and sifting through the catechisms of the LCMS?" Answer: These are the definitive textbooks that educate and so shape the theological context and interpretive outlook of the entire ministerium and every parishioner of our Synod. What these catechism explanations say has an impact on how we think, how we see, and how we live. And what our catechism says about the Third Commandment matters, because for several generations what is taught there has had a way of truncating all discussion and preempting any reflection on the meaning and significance of the commandment beyond the usual focused exhortation to faithful and attentive church attendance that comprised my own altogether typical childhood catechesis: "Go to church and pay attention." All this is to say that if I am to make any headway in broadening, deepening, heightening, and simply expanding the foundational significance and, I will argue, beauty of the sabbath commandment, then I must first take into account what Luther and our own catechism explanations have had to say about it. This accounts for the work of this chapter. With that task behind us, we are poised to get busy building an understanding of sabbath that sprouts in creation, blooms in redemption, and reaches fruition in the glory of eschatological consummation.

Before we tackle that work, let me be clear and reiterate that I have no interest in arguing with Luther! I do not disagree with his thinking about the sabbath or his explanations in either of his catechisms. Given his context and audience, his Small Catechism explanation of the commandment does exactly what it needed to do. And given the wider range of his exploration in the Large Catechism, he was obviously aware that there is more at work under the command than just the obligation to attend to God's Word—as important as that is. I am not the least interested in suggesting a tweak, much less a change, in the emphasis or wording of Luther's masterpiece that is his brief and beautiful Small Catechism. There is no need for that. I am, though, keenly intent on helping those who grew up with the Synod's catechism as the authoritative guide to their confession to come to an even fuller understanding and richer appreciation of all that is going on when God instructed Israel, "Remember the Sabbath day, by keeping it holy." It is certainly about much more than simply taking a day off from work each week, and as we will see, it is about even more than being sure to go to church and then paying careful attention during the sermon. Underneath these outward expressions of obedience to the ancient commandment lies a powerful and marvelous reality that defines the very core of our being and norms and directs the shape and direction of our living. In other words, the Third Commandment is not just for Israel of old; it is, instead, a very big deal capturing deep truth that undergirds and then blossoms and expands outward into every corner of God's eternal plan for his creation.

CHAPTER 2

SABBATH IN THE BIBLE

MORE THAN TIME OFF

One thing needs to be made clear from the beginning: God did not need to rest after six arduous days of creating the universe. God was not physically, spiritually, or emotionally taxed in the least—whatever those ascriptions might mean in relation to the omnipotent Creator. That God did choose to rest, and make a point of it, is indicative of something that must strike us as profoundly important; and this is exactly the way this idea is treated throughout the Bible. In other words, since God did not rest on the seventh day for his own benefit, his resting must have significance for the creation he made. And based on the Bible's own treatment of this rest, it seems that there is much more to it than merely a divine endorsement of a day off from work each week, as important as time off may be from a humanitarian or even economic standpoint. But what exactly is that profound importance? And how should we understand this idea of rest? Too often, it seems that God's resting on the seventh day is interpreted as essentially archetypical, and rest is understood primarily as inactivity. According to this view, God's seventh-day rest reveals the limits of man's nature and the regular, weekly need for recharging. Thus, the meaning of God's resting is reduced to "creatures should work for six days and take off the seventh"; and with that, the significance of God's Saturday rest has been exhausted. It is assumed that nothing more needs to be sought regarding the meaning of rest, besides teasing out the physical and spiritual components of what such required resting entails. But this is not the way that the Bible itself presents and treats the impact of God's day of rest.

Part of the difficulty we have in gaining a full appreciation of what the Bible does with God's resting on the seventh day is the word itself. We hear *rest* and we think of collapsing under a ponderosa pine after a long hike or stretching out on the couch after a long day at school. Rest is what people do in retirement homes. It's why we have vacations void of alarms and even clocks. A rest area is that designated spot along the highway where drivers can take a break from the road and truckers can catch a nap—the epitome of rest. And so rest comes to be defined in contrast to exertion, effort, and work whether physical, mental, or emotional. Rest is non-work, the antithesis of the concerted investment of resources, energy, and activity. Rest is typically associated with listless inactivity and even idleness. So, is that what it means to rest? Was it for the sake of sanctioning idle time free of labor that God rested on the seventh day? Is that the essence of the rest Jesus came to bring? While the idea of rest as inactivity is certainly not entirely foreign to the biblical picture of rest, there is in the Bible considerably more to God's first day of rest and the subsequent command to observe the sabbath day than only inactivity or a necessary period of refueling in order to replenish energies spent.

An exhaustive consideration of the entire Bible's treatment of seventh-day rest lies well beyond the scope of this little book, but there are a few critical places in the scriptural account that need our careful consideration if we are to appreciate rightly the tremendous importance of God's post-creation resting and the idea of sabbath rest that grows out of it and eventually achieves elite status within the Decalogue. We'll begin with the beginning, the beginning of the world itself and the beginning of the critical place of "resting" within God's plan.

THE RHYTHM OF CREATION

God took six days to create the universe. That is made painstakingly clear in the first creation account, which begins the Bible. No reason is given for the choice to create over the space of six days, and we neither can nor should speculate a reason. God simply did what he did the way he did it. Our existence and the lives we live are the result of his deliberate and intimately meticulous creative work as outlined in each of the creation accounts in the first two chapters of Genesis. The second narrative record makes no mention of the six days but does provide the rich story of the solicitous care with which God crafted the first man and woman and established them in his creation. That God crafted the entire universe over the course of six days is so well known that the peculiarity of the fact of a six-day creation may escape us. As many of the church fathers pointed out, an almighty being does not need any time to do what he decides to do. God could bring the entire universe into existence complete and whole with a single word requiring no time whatsoever.

By creating over the course of six successive days, God powerfully established the essential rhythm and cycles of time and life that would drive our world through its entire history. "There was evening and there was morning, one day."[1] And so it has continued since: the cycle of the day, the twenty-four-hour cadence that dictates and shapes our creatureliness. We are subject to the beat of each day. Indeed, our circadian rhythm is so much a part of our human nature that to ignore or resist it is to invite destruction of our very selves. With the sun we rise and embrace our work; and as the day turns to evening, we ease out of the efforts of the day and look with longing for the moment when we escape the world in sleep. Considered from the standpoint of our physical natures, rest is not needed one day in seven—it is needed roughly eight hours out of every twenty-four. That sort of rest is part of the daily pattern of life. Dietrich Bonhoeffer calls attention to this fundamental pattern for our lives, this "rhythm of the day," and hints at the problems

1 Genesis 1:5.

that ensue when we resist or even try to overcome the normative authority that the established rhythm holds over our lives.[2] What is clear in the creation account is that God's resting on day seven is something quite different than the human need for daily recharging through the rest of sleep.[3]

The creation account, then, establishes two rhythms: first is the natural rhythm of the twenty-four-hour day and then follows the pattern of the seven-day week. Interestingly, even those with no commitment to scriptural or theological truth must acknowledge the singular significance and oddity of the seven-day week. Days, months, and years all correspond to readily observable astronomical phenomena, so measuring time by sun and moon makes obvious sense. The standards are set by astronomical reality. But the week is not so neatly derived. Why seven days? Why not ten, or six (which divides nicely into 30), or five (which divides neatly into 365)? Some speculate that a week of seven days arose in conjunction with the approximate time between the various phases of the moon or the number of the five known-at-the-time planets plus the sun and moon; but there is no definitive ancient evidence to support the claims. The fact remains that the Bible's creation account stands as the single best explanation for what has become one of the essential rhythms of human lives: the week.

Seen in light of the Bible, the pattern of the week that seems so basic and natural to us is exactly that. It is part of the essential fabric of creation present since the beginning of the world. The world took shape over the course of the very first week. The week and the world are bound together in their very existence. The week, then, is part of nature itself. Of course, such a claim takes for granted the reliability and authority of the account in

2 Dietrich Bonhoeffer, *Creation and Fall* (New York: Touchstone, 1959), 28–29.

3 More about the significance of sleep will be considered in chapter 6.

Genesis as much more than an ancient "just so" story. By creating over six days and resting on the seventh, God founded the week. It was deliberate, an intentional part of his plan for this world. The weekly rhythm that directs and organizes our work, our play, our families, schools, and even churches is not an arbitrary arrangement or human construct but a reality built into the structure of the world itself, instituted from the very beginning.

Yet, while setting the pace for the rhythm of life should be recognized as an essential aspect of the seventh day of rest, which culminated and established the first week and all that would follow after, this truth does not yet capture the full significance of the fact that God chose to rest after completing the work of creation. There is more to God's actions on the seventh day than establishing the world's rhythm or endorsing the need for weekly rest. The key Hebrew verb used in the account already points in the direction of this richer meaning. "By the seventh day God completed His work which He had done, and He rested on the seventh day from all His work which He had done."[4] It is worth noting here that when God rested on the first seventh day, it was not called the sabbath. That particular word would come later—a product or outgrowth of the fundamental rest that God had established already at the end of creation week.[5]

The word translated *rest* in the creation account is *šābat*, and according to the definitive Old Testament theological dictionary,

4 Genesis 2:2.

5 For those accustomed to hearing and singing the liturgy, it may be worthwhile to offer a quick word of clarification. To praise "the Lord God of Sabaoth" in the Sanctus (*LSB*, p. 195) is not to acknowledge God as Lord of Sunday morning! *Sabaoth* is not a variant spelling of *sabbath*; they are not even related etymologically. *Sabbath*, of course, links to the word *šābat*, for *rest*, pointing to the seventh day when God rested from his work of creating. *Sabaoth*, on the other hand, is rooted in the Hebrew word for *host* or *army*, *sābā*. Yahweh Sabaoth, or the Lord God of Sabaoth, is a reference to God as the leader of armies and has nothing to do with a day of worship or God resting.

it means "cease, come to an end," which offers a slightly different nuance than just "rest." But the word also has the specialized meaning of "celebrate."[6] In other words, the point is not that God caught his breath or stretched out for a bit but simply that he stopped doing the work of creating his world. The job was done—completed exactly as God had planned. Of course it was. We know this sense of completion in a dim sort of way when we wrap up some project that has occupied our effort. The grass has been cut, the borders edged, and the sidewalks swept clean. The job is done, the workers stop working, they rest; and unlike God, they do need to catch their breath. But, like any good work of creation or even preservation, when the job is done, there is that sweet shot of satisfaction—not only is the work finished, but the results are spot-on: the lawn looks great, the car's finish reflects light like a mirror, the house is clean and the meal spread on the table, the new paint on the nursery wall is perfect. The rest from the work is attended by a deep moment of heartfelt celebration over a job well done.

THE FOUNDATION OF THE CELEBRATION

So, to say that God rested has nothing at all to do with the Creator collapsing exhausted, his energies spent. It has everything to do with God marking the completion of his extraordinary masterpiece. God sets aside an entire day simply to soak in the sheer joy and delight of the perfection he had accomplished. He takes a day to survey and relish the height and depth, the enormity and intricacy, the abundance and beauty of his entire remarkable universe. Wrapped up in his resting, then, is a sharp

6 *Theological Dictionary of the Old Testament*, revised edition, vol. I–XV, eds. G. Johannes Botterweck, Helmer Ringgren, and Heinz-Josef Fabry, trans. J. T. Willis, G. W. Bromiley, D. E. Green, and D. W. Stott (Grand Rapids: Eerdmans, 1977–2012), s.v. "šābat."

sense of delight in the detail, festivity at the completion, and joy over the achievement of his plan. In fact, these are the dominant and most important aspects of God's sanctification of the seventh day. He set it apart to celebrate what had been accomplished. That God rested meant that he surveyed all that he had made, pronounced it complete and very good, and then spent a day reveling in the splendid wonder of it all. On the seventh day, God did not flop down in his recliner or crash in the shade; he celebrated what had been accomplished and delighted in what he had made. Resting is not pulling back from the creation; it is not the cessation of God's involvement with the world he had made. It is quite the opposite, in fact. God resting on the final day of the first week means that the work of creating, culminating in the creation of man, was complete and fulfilled exactly as he had intended. All had been accomplished, and God was delighted with his work.

This is the foundation for the sabbath commands that eventually follow but that don't actually appear until the time of Moses. The people are instructed to gather a double portion of manna on day six so that they will be able to honor the next day, the sabbath. That's the first mention of the word in the Bible.[7] But it is not the children of Israel in the wilderness who are the first people to celebrate a sabbath. That distinction falls to Adam and Eve. Created by God on day six, the first full day of their existence would have been on the seventh day, the day that God rests. The Creator shares his celebration day with the first man and the first woman. They begin their lives on the earth and in the garden joining their Creator in reveling over the sheer wonder of the world and the myriad relationships between the God who created and his universe jammed full of

7 Exodus 16:23.

the wonders he had made. This truth must not be missed: the man and woman have yet to work a full day in the garden God gave them to tend, but already they are observing the first day of rest with God. They have no work or accomplishments of their own to consider but only the work of God.[8] The day of rest stands, then, at the very beginning of human existence. It is the sacred time that marks the reality of the whole creation at the height of its fullness and beauty. God celebrates his creation. The stewards of his creation, the first man and woman, Adam and Eve, celebrate with him. It is the first true holy day, a day set apart, a day of celebration, a genuine holiday in the richest possible sense of the word.

This is the great truth of the seventh day. It is the day when creation relishes what it means to be living just the way that God had intended. All the parts of creation are working perfectly together, each in its own peculiar place and with its own specific way fitting together in a marvelously interconnected, mutual interdependence exactly as God planned it. Every creature is doing what God had put it in the world to do. There is joy and there is harmony and there is deep and profound peace that together engulf and suffuse the myriad parts of creation. Creator and creation are living according to God's good plan. And Adam and Eve are right in the middle of it all, celebrating with God. This is the underlying context for what will eventually one day be called the Third Commandment. With every one of the Ten Commandments, the specific, positive declaration or articulation spelled out in the commandment is simply the presentation of a deep-seated truth grounded in the very foundations of the

8 This is an insight made, along with a wealth of other profound observations about the creation account, in Karl Barth, *Church Dogmatics*, vol. 3, *The Doctrine of Creation*, part 1, eds. G. W. Bromiley and T. F. Torrance (Edinburgh: T&T Clark, 1958), 217ff.

creation itself. So, for example, the command to have no other gods is not merely a warning to Israel to shun the polytheism of surrounding pagan nations; more fully, the commandment spells out the truth that only God is God and that every creature must naturally acknowledge God's lordship over all of creation. Similarly, the command not to misuse the name of the Lord is not exhausted by substituting "the Lord" for every instance of "YHWH" when reading the Hebrew text, nor by avoiding cursing in God's name. The Second Commandment reminds us of the truth that every creature must offer the Creator, whose name is Yahweh, appropriate honor and praise.

So, what is the foundational truth at work underneath the command to remember the sabbath day? Certainly, it is about much more than knocking off from the daily drudgery of the job every seventh day. And there is even more going on than the obviously important need to hear and heed God's Word attentively and regularly as the Small Catechism stresses. The Third Commandment prohibiting work on the sabbath day points to the greater reality first celebrated on the world's first seventh day: God and creation in a right relationship with one another and all of creation functioning together in perfect rhythm and harmony in a beautiful masterpiece that delights both God and each individual creature. The sabbath day was established to ensure that human creatures would remember and celebrate the wonder of all God had wrought when he created—not the least of which was the abiding joy that attends human life when lived in a right relationship with God and creation. The connection between the command to keep the sabbath and the first day of divine rest and celebration at the end of creation week is made explicit when God gives Moses the law at Sinai, including, of course, the first articulation of the Decalogue:

> Remember the sabbath day, to keep it holy. Six days you shall labor and do all your work, but the seventh day is a sabbath of the LORD your God: in it you shall not do any work, you or your son or your daughter, your male or your female servant or your cattle or your sojourner who stays with you. For in six days the LORD made the heavens and the earth, the sea and all that is in them, and rested on the seventh day; therefore the LORD blessed the sabbath day and made it holy.[9]

In Deuteronomy, when the entire Decalogue is repeated and renewed ahead of Israel's conquest of Canaan, the second giving of the command to keep the sabbath is tied to God's work in the exodus itself:

> Observe the sabbath day to keep it holy, as the LORD your God commanded you. Six days you shall labor and do all your work, but the seventh day is a sabbath of the LORD your God; in it you shall not do any work, you or your son or your daughter or your male servant or your female servant or your ox or your donkey or any of your cattle or your sojourner who stays with you, so that your male servant and your female servant may rest as well as you. You shall remember that you were a slave in the land of Egypt, and the LORD your God brought you out of there by a

9 Exodus 20:8–11.

> mighty hand and by an outstretched arm; therefore the LORD your God commanded you to observe the sabbath day.[10]

Clearly there are differences in the two accounts, the most significant being that the first giving of the command grounds the sabbath observance in the creation story, while the second grounds it in Israel's liberation from Egyptian slavery. Both accounts, however, are otherwise remarkably consistent; the second provides only a slight embellishment with "ox and donkey" listed along with "all cattle." Both accounts provide an extensive listing of those who are required to keep the commandment, and both leave no doubt that this command prescribes when it is right to work and when one must not work. And this latter fact is rather a significant point because it seems at first blush to blunt and invalidate all that I've been suggesting and arguing about the true meaning and importance of the commandment. But that is precisely the point.

THE EXPRESSION OF THE COMMANDMENT

There is an obvious surface level to the command: no Israelite—and no non-Israelite living in the community and not even any domestic animal—is to do any work on the sabbath. That's the self-evident message of the commandment. And yet, it is also clear that this command was to be observed not for its own sake, as if taking a day off had inherent significance or unleashed untold spiritual blessings. There is nothing magical or even necessarily spiritual about taking a day off from work. The point of the command not to work was to remind Israel of God's creation and God's redemption. He made them and he saved them. God's creation established their identity and their place in

10 Deuteronomy 5:12–15.

the world; and God's redemption put them back into that special relationship not only with him but even with all of creation, a truth made manifest in the Promised Land of Canaan, which was designated as the place for God's people to thrive. Keeping the sabbath was meant to point to those twin realities. Not working was not the point. Remembering, sanctifying, honoring, and celebrating God's glorious work on behalf of his people and simply resonating with and delighting in the lingering wonder of that great work of creation and redemption was the point. The startling, intrusive, and schedule-jarring practice of calling a halt to human activity and stopping all work every sabbath would serve as an appropriate and poignant trigger to point the people to remember the centrality of God's own rest on day seven, when he stopped his work of creating, surveyed all that he had done, and rejoiced in all that he saw. Not working on the sabbath is certainly consistent with the observance of such a day, but it is hardly the bottom line or most important part of the day.

Thus, I would argue that while the outward form of the commandment was focused on a determination to ensure that no work would be done each sabbath, the much wider and more important point was that each and every sabbath was to remind Israel to recognize and live in the truth of the delightful rest practiced by God on the first seventh day. It was the rich, wonderful, comprehensive, celebratory rest of all of creation in sync, as planned. In other words, each part of creation is in perfect harmony with itself, with the rest of creation, and with God the Creator. The abrupt stoppage of work each sabbath should have aimed the people to see the greater truth that was at work under the command to cease activity and so lead them to participate in God's rest like the first man and woman had done so long ago when the world was but six days old. This is a rest far more profound than a day off to recharge physically and spiritually—this is the rest of creation delighting in the zenith, the highest culmination, of its very reason for being. This is creation doing what it was created to do and rejoicing in the superabundant and always-new gifts of God.

While a host of additional observations and comments could be offered on this pair of texts and the significance of the twofold delivery of the Third Commandment, two deserve particular mention here. First, it should be noticed that both expressions of what we number as the Third Commandment, fully cited above, include the second longest expansion of any of the Ten Commandments. Only the extended elaboration on the First Commandment—with the prohibitions against graven images and the "I, the Lord your God, am a jealous God" section, which Luther extracts and repositions after the final commandment—is longer. Naturally, it makes sense that the First Commandment would receive extra attention. It is the normative commandment that directs all that follow. One must know God as God and acknowledge his authority as Creator and Lord over all to make sense of the rest of the Decalogue. But, why the extensive elaboration on the Third Commandment? What makes it so special? The best explanation is again that this commandment carries singular importance. It is special.

That the Third Commandment was intended to be exhaustive and comprehensive in application is made extravagantly clear: son, daughter, male and female servants, ox, donkey, any cattle, and sojourners are all included on the list. We are tempted to declare: "All right, everyone and everything needs to rest, we get the point!" But do we? I would argue that the point is not that everyone gets a day off or that we all need time to rest. In the context of the original creation account and in light of this long list of creatures, the point of this Decalogue commandment for sabbath observance is the fact that it is meant to be a creation-wide observance centered on the wonder, beauty, and joy of God's work for the sake of Israel and the whole creation without exception. None are left out. All are participants in God's creative plan, and all enjoy the goodness of living in step with God's plan.

Seen in this light, we recognize that the commandment is aimed not only at creatures rightly observing and celebrating an in-sync relationship between God and the individual; it is also aimed at leading the creature to delight in every relationship between each individual creature and all the rest of creation around him. In other words, the Third Commandment touches both the vertical (God-focused) and the horizontal (creation-focused) relationships of creatures. This matters for the simple reason that the commandment is almost universally considered to be part of "the first table" of the law. Therefore, it is assumed that the Third Commandment relates to a creature's vertical relationship with God without having much to do with that creature's relationships with other creatures on the horizontal plane. It is as if the Third Commandment is some arbitrary rule God contrived primarily to make Israel odd and, perhaps more beneficently, to enshrine the ideal of time off from work. But the elaborately comprehensive nature of the command points in the direction of creation itself and serves to remind us that the point of the command is God, along with all of the creatures he made, living in right relationships with one another. Perhaps we should no longer think of the Third Commandment as a strange, Israel-specific commandment that concludes the God-relations part of the Decalogue, the "first table." Maybe, instead, the commandment should be seen as the bridge commandment that leads us from the normative centrality of God and his holy name to the peace and harmony God originally intended for his people and all of creation, a harmony or shalom that is then given concrete content and direction in the succeeding seven commandments.

The second point worth noting about these twin commands to keep the sabbath is that both emphasize that the work being done in advance of the sabbath is being done by God. In other words, the context for each sabbath command (that is, creation and exodus respectively) situates the celebration in the context of the work God has done for his creatures. Creatures are but recipients and benefactors. God acts; creatures receive. It was already observed that for the first man and woman, the seventh day of rest, what we might anachronistically call the first sabbath day, coincided with their first full day of life. On that first day of rest, they had not yet done anything. Adam and Eve "rested" before they had had time to do anything more in their new garden home than a quick orientation tour strolling around the grounds. God was the one who worked; he had done *all* the work. Nevertheless, God invited the freshly created man and woman to share in the joyful celebration with him. He wanted them to be part of the festivities, delighting in what had been done.

The same theme is reinforced, perhaps even more emphatically, in the Deuteronomy version of the commandment. Recall that in this renewal of the covenant law, the command to keep the sabbath is premised on the people remembering their Egyptian bondage and the unilateral action of God to free them from slavery. They had been slaves—utterly helpless and, truth be told, utterly hopeless. It took the people of Israel almost as long to come to terms with the reality of God's plan as it did

Pharaoh. They were skeptical and almost reluctant recipients of grace. God did the work of rescuing, reclaiming, and restoring his people while they simply watched in awe and learned to believe and rejoice—which, as noted, took a while; the sins of doubt and disbelief are not easily renounced or relinquished. The people did nothing; the people could do nothing. God did what needed to be done. God worked their salvation. They were the objects and recipients of his concerted activity to thwart Pharaoh and all of Egypt and to redeem and honor the people he had chosen.

The point in both the Exodus and the Deuteronomy versions of the Third Commandment is the same, and it is plainly evident. But, while there is no mystery surrounding the obvious point of creaturely passivity in the reception of the sabbath gift, this patent truth is rarely received with the enthusiasm it deserves. Both texts emphasize that humans are contingent, passive receivers of what God alone can give. Remembering and embracing this dependent reality with appropriate humility, gratitude, and praise is a critical part of what it means, then, for humans to keep the sabbath day. Once again, we see that infinitely more is going on in the keeping of the sabbath day than merely a studied determination not to do anything that might be construed as work.

LEARNING TO DELIGHT

From the outset, and throughout the Old Testament, sabbath-keeping is intended to be a rich delight in the work God has done, an invitation for God's people to acknowledge what God has completed by giving him their exclusive worship. And yet, even more profoundly and wonderfully, the giving of the sabbath command is God's personal invitation for his creatures to join him in his celebration of the creation: the Creator bidding each creature made in his image, and all the rest of creation in every corner of the vast universe, to be swept up in a thriving, dynamic, vibrant harmony that relishes together what it means to be God's handiwork, a vital part of God's extraordinary work of creation, redemption, and full restoration. So it is that every sabbath is not just a looking back at what God has done; it is also a looking forward with confidence to what he will soon bring to full completion on the great Last Day, when his eternal plan is finally and fully realized. All of this is present and at work on every sabbath day. The sabbath is so important, so central to living life well, that sabbath observance is commanded in the Decalogue itself. But, it should by now be clear that so much more is going on than just a prohibition against creatures doing any work; observing the sabbath is preeminently about God and his gracious, perfect work for the sake of his creatures.

Every sabbath day occurs in the context of the first day of rest on the very first seventh day. In that light, every sabbath should be a day of profound joy and rich celebration, a day to delight in the sheer wonder of God's grace given to his whole creation. Hiking above the tree line at sunrise, wading in the quiet surf at sunset, strolling beneath a canopy of autumn leaves dappled by the noon sun, friends gathered around the embers of a dying campfire, or family gathered near the tree on Christmas Eve—all capture some aspect of the nature of this celebration of God's good gift of creation. It is life full, sweet, rich, and wonderful in and with creation as God intended it. It is a beautiful image—but life does not always work that way, of course. Far too often, far too many people (in truth, all people at one time or another) can consider this idyllic imagery of life at its very best as little more than a mocking farce, a distant fiction smothered by a painful, ugly, unrelenting reality that makes talk of joy, delight, and celebration seem a naïve fairytale or a saccharine charade. We see the anguished misery, hear the sobbing groans, smell the decaying rot, taste the acrid bitterness, and suffer the crushing agony. All people know the sorrow and affliction inflicted by sin, suffering, and death—some people seem to know it more intensely and consistently than others, but none are immune. And yet, in spite of this harsh reality—indeed, precisely to confront and remedy this cruel reality—the stalwart command to celebrate sabbath persists.

God does not, however, just reiterate the command. He advances his plan, and we encounter a new and remarkable turn in God's plan that changes everything: we witness the coming of the Christ, the arrival and the work of Jesus. Luke recounts the deliciously dramatic moment when this new chapter was first revealed to the world.

THE SABBATH INCARNATE

Jesus lived most of his life among the people of Nazareth. They were his people; related to one another by more than geography or economy, they were bound by blood. Numbering not more than a few hundred people, Nazareth was literally a large extended family—more like a typical rural congregation than a small town. Jesus had grown up in the hilltop village, decidedly off the beaten track, where everyone knew everyone else and where minding one's own business was an empirical impossibility. This makes Jesus' stunning sabbath-day declaration in the Nazareth synagogue and the subsequent reaction all the more remarkable. Since Luke also records the story of Jesus' visit to Jerusalem when he was twelve, these are not the first words of Jesus recorded in this gospel, but they are the first of his adult ministry. It seems clear that Luke so arranges his account specifically to make a point. In Matthew's gospel, Jesus visits his hometown of Nazareth and preaches in his old synagogue in chapter 13, well into his active ministry and after he has already preached the Sermon on the Mount and done numerous miracles. Luke is quite aware of Jesus' work that preceded his visit to Nazareth, noting that after Jesus' baptism and wilderness trial by the tempter, Jesus "returned to Galilee in the power of the Spirit and news about Him spread through all the surrounding district. And He began teaching in their synagogues and was praised by all."[11] But Luke offers no detail about this public inauguration of Jesus' ministry. Luke chooses instead to focus on what happens in Nazareth; more specifically, Luke's focus is not on a particular action per se, but on a speech. Luke begins his account of Jesus' ministry by centering all attention on what Jesus says to the people of Nazareth.

It seems that Jesus was more or less expected to preach that day, a fitting and expedient gesture on the part of the synagogue official tasked with "filling the pulpit" each week. To have the newly appeared rabbi, the very one creating a minor sensation in the land, read the text and preach to his home congregation was a scheduling triumph. A packed house was all but guaranteed. And the provocative young rabbi did not disappoint. Handed the Isaiah scroll, Jesus chose his own text from what we today would call chapter 61, with a bit of helpful embellishment from chapter 58:

> The Spirit of the Lord is upon Me, because He anointed Me to preach the gospel to the poor. He has sent Me to proclaim release to the captives,

11 Luke 4:14–15.

> and recovery of sight to the blind, to set free those who are oppressed, to proclaim the favorable year of the Lord.[12]

The ancient text from the great prophet pointed to that longed-for day when Yahweh's chosen and anointed servant would arrive to bring God's kingdom, to proclaim the favorable year of the Lord, to inaugurate the ultimate year of jubilee. The idea of the jubilee year had been established already in the days of Moses. It was part of the Levitical code. The year-long observance was to come after a week of a week of years, that is, seven sets of seven years, or in other words, forty-nine years. The next year, the fiftieth, was the jubilee year, when the tilled land would lie fallow—resting; all indentured servants were set free, all debts were canceled, and all property reverted back once more to the original ancestral family owners. Scholars debate whether Israel ever actually observed the jubilee year as directed; but we know without doubt that about seven centuries after Moses, Isaiah saw the coming of the Messiah as the inauguration of the ultimate jubilee year for all people for all time. No wonder the people of Jesus' day dreamed of the coming of the Messiah, who would finally and forever make right all that was wrong in the broken creation. Their yearning for the Messiah, for the final jubilee, was palpable.

Given this context, when Jesus matter-of-factly declares to that sabbath crowd in Nazareth, "Today this Scripture has been fulfilled in your hearing,"[13] it was an astonishing, legitimately mind-blowing claim. Of course, Jesus fully intended to announce nothing less than all that his incredible claim implied.

12 Luke 4:18–19.
13 Luke 4:21.

He was proclaiming himself to be the Messiah, to be the very advent of jubilee itself. On that sabbath day, he declared himself to be the living, present embodiment of sabbath: God and all of creation in perfect harmony as God had always planned. It was God in human flesh, Jesus himself, who brought the restoration. Jesus *was* the restoration. He was the sabbath reality. It was a staggering revelation and an audacious assertion.

The people, for their part, would have none of it. All of Jesus' fellow townspeople—the friends, the relatives, the people with whom he had shared all of his life—categorically rejected his claim. They could not believe it . . . or more accurately, they would not believe it. The reasons for their rejection are implicit in the text: Jesus was just too familiar, too ordinary, too much like them to be the long-awaited Messiah. Jesus' outrageous declaration was crazy, offensive, and wholly unbelievable. But in the face of their incredulity, Jesus does not flinch and drives his point home with even more intensity, leaving the infuriated townspeople on the verge of lynching their most famous son. The day's events established what would become a familiar pattern as the world came face to face with its Messiah; it is a pattern that holds to the present. John put it this way: "He came to His own, and those who were His own did not receive Him."[14] Those who should have known Jesus and received him rejected him. Never was this truer than that sabbath in Nazareth.

The degree of the rejection is highlighted all the more in Mark's gospel. Mark recounts for us the earlier story of that awkward moment when Jesus' mother and brothers came seeking an audience with Jesus only to have him declare that all those who do the will of God are his mother and brothers. What should not be missed is that the kinsmen of Jesus, or "His own people,"

14 John 1:11.

who were waiting at the threshold hoping to see Jesus, had actually come "to take custody of Him; for they were saying, 'He has lost His senses.'"[15] It seems that the townspeople of Nazareth had passed their judgment on the legitimacy of Jesus' ministry long before he arrived in town to preach on that sabbath. In the gospels of Mark and Matthew, the story of Jesus' embarrassed family trying to protect their crazy relative from himself is followed within a chapter or two with the account of the Nazareth rejection. The same players, the same childhood acquaintances and relatives, were likely involved. Jesus' ministry had a way of upsetting the usual arrangements.

Jesus' proclivity for upsetting the carefully achieved status quo of first-century Judaism is no secret. And it is in that spirit that we are usually taught to read the frequent sabbath controversies that arise in the Gospels. On any given sabbath, it seems, Jesus is bound to encounter someone who needs help: a man with dropsy or a woman bent double. In the face of such suffering, he summarily heals what is ruined in spite of the explicit rabbinical rules forbidding such actions, rules assiduously followed by the Pharisees, of course. On the face of it, Jesus seems to be making the point that he gets to decide what laws he will or will not follow when it comes to caring for his people. Or in a more independent-minded spirit, we might see this behavior of Jesus as a declaration that restrictive rules don't matter and that the days of straitjacketed sabbath-keeping obsessed with doing nothing that might be construed as work are gone, along with any other laws that seem to impinge on human happiness. No doubt, there is in these events an element of Jesus asserting his divine authority to make and break laws as he chooses. We may even be able to grant a certain measure of the establishment of Christian liberty as Jesus goes about redefining the lives of those

15 Mark 3:21.

who would faithfully follow in God's will. But the truth is that in the Gospels there is more going on with these sabbath confrontations than merely "Jesus versus the Pharisees" and even more than Jesus as the champion of freedom from the law. The bigger, more important point is what Jesus teaches all of us about sabbath as God intended it to be. This is a particularly strong aspect in Luke's gospel.

ALL THAT SABBATH IS MEANT TO BE

After Jesus successfully departs Nazareth and the homicidal crowd, simply "passing through their midst," Luke, in the very next verse, tells us about another sabbath, this one in Capernaum. On this sabbath, Jesus has a very full day. First, he heals a man "possessed by the spirit of an unclean demon," a spirit who had made a loud and accurate declaration of Jesus' identity as "the Holy One of God!" Leaving the synagogue, Jesus goes to Simon Peter's home, where he heeds the request of those present and intervenes on behalf of Peter's mother-in-law suffering from a high fever, who, quite interestingly, "immediately got up" after she had been healed "and waited on them." Apparently, she was also working on the sabbath for the sake of Jesus. Finally, that same day, "while the sun was setting, all those who had any who were sick with various diseases brought them to Him; and laying His hands on each one of them, He was healing them."[16] Jesus' ministry is in full swing, he is pushing back the darkness of Satan's reign, overturning the suffering disease that marked life in the sin-riddled creation and sending people back into their vocations to do the things God had given them to do. And, of course, he is doing all of this on the sabbath, because all of this is exactly what sabbath was always meant to be.

Luke's juxtaposition of the Nazareth sabbath and the

16 Luke 4:31–40.

Capernaum sabbath is highly significant and drives home the point that Jesus is not only the one who sets the rules for the sabbath but he is the bringer and the very presence of sabbath. Luke carefully positioned the Nazareth proclamation at the very beginning of Jesus' ministry. There Jesus declares that he is the arrival of the jubilee, the living embodiment, the ultimate fulfillment and celebration of the sabbath. And from the moment of this pronouncement, Luke tells a succession of stories of Jesus doing exactly what he declared in his hometown. These sabbath stories are spread throughout Luke's gospel; no other evangelist has more. The word *sabbath* occurs seventeen times in Luke; Mark comes in second among the four gospels with eleven uses of the word. Jesus' relation to the sabbath is a key aspect of Luke's telling of the story of Jesus.

Luke's keen interest in the sabbath picks up again only a couple chapters after the stories of Nazareth and Capernaum where the evangelist recounts two separate sabbaths back-to-back. This time, sabbath is not only the setting but also the topic of intense conversation. After being harangued by some Pharisees for allowing his disciples to snack on some freshly picked and winnowed wheat on a sabbath, Jesus reminds them of their ancestor David's liberties taken with the consecrated bread and concludes his rebuttal with the assertion: "The Son of Man is Lord of the Sabbath."[17] That Luke uses the imperfect tense gives the sense that this was not a one and done statement of Jesus but a declaration he made repeatedly. To declare Jesus as Lord of the sabbath brings with it all the entailments of the Lord who first created and then celebrated his creation with a day of delightful resting. Jesus is that Lord, David's greater Lord, the Lord who does not need to observe rabbinic restrictions in order to hallow the day, but who fully consecrates the

17 Luke 6:5.

day merely by his presence in it. He brings the holiness of sabbath—harmony between Creator and creatures and within all creation—everywhere he goes. He is the fulfillment of sabbath, the Lord of sabbath.

The second sabbath story in chapter 6 of Luke recounts yet another collision between Jesus, the bringer of sabbath wholeness, and the Pharisees, who are wholly committed to making sabbath holy by their own actions—or more accurately, *in*actions. Once again, we watch Jesus act with calculated deliberation not only to assert his lordship of the sabbath but also to demonstrate what sabbath entails: doing good and saving lives, making whole and restoring what is impotent and useless. In this case, Jesus celebrates sabbath joy by fully restoring a man who languished with a withered hand. Such an ineffective hand would make life hard and make doing profitable work even harder, but the impediment would not kill him. And that's precisely the reason for the healing: the saving that Jesus brings extends to all of life and aims at making life rich and fruitful and joyful as God had intended. In these sabbath cases, Jesus is not pulling people from the jaws of death or helping them merely to survive—they had learned the tactics necessary for just getting by long ago. No, Jesus brings sabbath by making creatures complete and whole, bringing them into the fullness of life so that they can also join in the celebration of God's good creation as full participants. That is sabbath work. That is the work that Jesus does.

Luke's gospel contains two more sabbath interactions between Jesus and those intent on consecrating the sabbath with their own fastidious rule-keeping. In chapter 13, it is Jesus, once again, who initiates the healing. He notices a woman bent over from some debilitating affliction. Obviously, this affliction is not a health crisis necessitating an immediate healing to cheat imminent death. And no one in the synagogue, not even the woman, thought it appropriate to ask Jesus to intervene. Perhaps everyone, including the broken woman herself, had become so accustomed to this sorry state of affairs that it simply seemed normal—certainly nothing to warrant a miraculous act of healing from Jesus. But Jesus sees the situation—rather, he sees the suffering woman—quite differently. Calling her to himself, he immediately announces, "Woman, you are freed from your sickness," lays his hands on her, and she stands upright for the first time in eighteen years. On cue, the local ruler of the synagogue, the local ruler of sabbath decrees, issues a new congregational policy: "There are six days in which work should be done; so come during them and get healed, and not on the Sabbath day."[18] But, of course, what this man saw as a common-sense solution to the problem of sabbath healing, Jesus exposes as blatant hypocrisy. This narrow legalism is a violation of everything that the sabbath means. When sabbath comes, creation is restored. When sabbath comes, a bent-over woman must stand straight and tall, a withered hand must be healed, a possessed soul must be freed. Releasing God's people from the bonds of sin and suffering and Satan is precisely the point of sabbath. Again, Jesus makes good on his Nazareth declaration. He turns the captives loose and cuts the bonds of those imprisoned. He thwarts the misery of hell and breaks the bond of Satan, and he does it all on the sabbath. Of course, he does it on the sabbath! He is, after all, the Lord of the sabbath—the one who brings to his creation, the one who is himself the very embodiment of, the fullness, the wonder, the sheer delight and celebration that is the heart of sabbath.

Luke's final sabbath story comes just one chapter later, and in many ways it is the least dramatic of them all. It is the

18 Luke 13:10–17.

familiar pattern with a slight twist: this time Jesus and the Pharisees are together on a sabbath, not in a synagogue for worship but in a home for dinner. A man with dropsy is there, and yet again, Jesus makes the first move. Whether or not the broken man had been planted in the gathering as one more test of Jesus' obedience and piety is immaterial. Jesus sees the need and does exactly what is expected; he seizes the opportunity to bring healing—of course he does. But not just yet. Before he heals, Jesus turns his attention away from the afflicted man for just a moment to address his silent, censorious critics who are watching and waiting for Jesus to act. It seems that everyone knows exactly what is about to happen. But before taking the action everyone rightly expects, Jesus asks a question, the one question that mattered: "Is it lawful to heal on the Sabbath, or not?"[19]

The answer, the answer none of the Pharisees could conceive, is of course a resounding "Yes!" Jesus does not heal in spite of the law. He heals in conformity with the law. It was always the law's purpose to uphold and enhance the harmony, the delight, the celebration of sabbath. To heal what is broken in creation and make it whole again is not antithetical to sabbath; it is the essence of sabbath. Jesus was not flouting the law of God; he was perfectly fulfilling it. The Pharisees simply could not grasp the grace and glory that were inherent in the sabbath. It is not only the life-threatening need of an ox or a son who falls into a well that requires sabbath intervention; it is the nature of sabbath itself that requires doing any and all work that brings about the healing of the creation and the restoration of God's world—including making a man with dropsy whole again. Breaking the awkward silence among the gathered dinner guests, Jesus heals the man and leaves his detractors shamed or perhaps

19 Luke 14:3.

just baffled into continued silence. And the evangelist Luke himself has no more sabbath words either—none until he relates one last sabbath story, the one about that long, sad sabbath before the stunning re-creation and restoration of *every*thing in creation on Easter morning.

In Luke, we see seamless continuity with the Old Testament beginnings of sabbath. Jesus comes, Luke makes clear, to bring sabbath to glorious fruition, to bring God's sabbath to splendid and joyful completion. Jesus comes to bring the jubilee forever. The sabbath celebration that had been obscured and perverted by overly zealous protectors of God's sabbath was made whole and beautiful again. Jesus saves sabbath by saving the world. To do one is to do the other; the ideas are synonymous. In Luke's account, Jesus does not attack the sabbath rules because he is opposed to the law; he rejects the rabbinic rules because their rules are opposed to the law. To save the world, Jesus does not reject the law; he keeps the law. He lives and fulfills all that sabbath was always meant to be. In Luke, Jesus declares that he is the Lord of the sabbath, the Creator and Redeemer of sabbath. And as the fulfillment of the ancient prophecy recorded by Isaiah, Jesus brings what sabbath was in the beginning and was always supposed to be: joyful harmony, resting in the wonder of creation, celebrating the delight of God's work—in a word, jubilee. People can resist, reject, and do their best to thwart the sabbath, but they cannot stop it. They cannot stop Jesus. He comes and he brings sabbath to his world again. He comes and he brings the promise of the ultimate, eternal sabbath yet to come.

THE SABBATH STILL TO COME

Having considered briefly the beginning of the idea of sabbath rest in a few critical portions of the Old Testament and then seeing how Jesus extends, elevates, and embodies the place of that rest in God's plan for his creation, it remains to think for a bit about where sabbath fits in the biblical story's end. The author of Hebrews does exactly that for us.

Hebrews is a unique book in the canon. The author is anonymous; it is the longest general epistle (longer than even Paul's second letter to the Corinthians); and though it is grouped with the epistles, it is much more like a sermon. It is also tightly bound to the Old Testament in style and subject. The pericope immediately relevant to our study of sabbath rest comes in chapter 4. Toward the end of Hebrews 3, the unnamed preacher had leveled a stern warning: "Take care, brethren, that there not be in any one of you an evil, unbelieving heart that falls away from the living God." Then, to sharpen the point, the reader is reminded of faithless Israel, "whose bodies fell in the wilderness" and who heard God declare "that they would not enter His rest."[20] Thus the author of Hebrews serves up the critical word *rest* once again. What is fascinating and important in this text's mention of rest is that it is the Promised Land of Canaan—or more accurately, life lived in the land of promise—that is specifically named as God's rest. This helps reaffirm the move this entire present chapter on sabbath has been making to push out the meaning of rest much more broadly than merely inactivity or the even more constrained idea of rest as simply an antonym for work. Rest is the realization and celebration of God's promise; it is life in the Promised Land.

But the writer to the Hebrews was not the first to make this broader connection of rest to the joy of living in God's delightful country flowing with milk and honey. Given his thick connections to the heritage of Israel, it comes as no surprise that the unnamed author of Hebrews quotes from the Old Testament; he

20 Hebrews 3:12, 17–18.

does so regularly. In our present text, he cites Psalm 95, a great song of praise, which has found a liturgical home as the Venite in the church's order of Matins. The psalm exalting God's lordship over all creation and his tender care for his chosen sheep ends, not atypically for a psalm, with a rather discordant, harsh warning: do not be like the people of Moses' day who erred "in their heart" and did not know God's ways. The Creator's disgust with that faithless generation is captured potently in the psalm's final verse: "Therefore I swore in My anger, truly they shall not enter into My rest."[21] This is the verse quoted in Hebrews 4:3.

Without a doubt, the warning against unbelief remains valid today and still deserves to be heeded, but the point of particular interest for the writer to the Hebrews and for us is that in Psalm 95, God's rest was equated with living in the land flowing with milk and honey. God's rest was the description of people living in the fulfillment of God's promises. God's rest was the goal of the exodus. And yet, even as the psalmist is the first biblical writer to equate explicitly the Promised Land with God's rest, when the psalmist exhorts his readers to obedience, he implicitly points ahead, as the writer of Hebrews makes clear, to yet another rest still to come. The psalmist admonishes: "Today, if you would hear His voice, do not harden your hearts, as at Meribah . . . when your fathers tested Me."[22] In other words, the psalmist knows that for his own readers there remains a promised rest still waiting ahead for them even though they are already living in Canaan.

This is the key point, and the writer of Hebrews jumps on it. For his own readers, yes even for us, there is also a promised rest that still lies ahead, one that we must not squander and forfeit through unbelief. The driving argument of Hebrews chapter 4, in

---

21 Psalm 95:10–11.

22 Psalm 95:7–9.

addition to the warning against missing out on God's rest, is that there is even more to God's rest than merely living in the Holy Land. God's rest, the rest of Genesis and Exodus, along with the rest of Psalm 95 and Hebrews 3 and 4, should be understood as the verbal and conceptual signifier for the goal of all human life. In the stern admonition of Hebrews 4—aimed now at his Christian readers—not to fall short of entering God's rest, the rest is obviously not Canaan and not simply a typical Saturday's day off from work. The rest highlighted as the goal in Hebrews 4 can only be the eternal rest of God's eschatological restoration on the day of Christ's return. Here, rest must mean the consummation of the creation at the final resurrection.

What is particularly interesting about this fully ripened understanding of God's rest in Hebrews is that the connection to the creation account is overtly emphasized to the point of being heavy-handed. The full text of Hebrews 4:3 reads: "For we who have believed enter that rest, just as He has said, 'As I swore in My wrath, they shall not enter My rest,' although His works were finished from the foundation of the world." The reference to the foundation of the world seems to be inserted for no other reason than to help establish the creational setting for a full and rich understanding of rest. Having made the point that the preaching of good news must be met with faith, the writer doubles down on the continuity of the rest he has in mind by invoking the very first rest of the creation account. He directly quotes Genesis 2:2: "And God rested on the seventh day from all His works."[23] The word for rest used in Hebrews is *katapauō*, the same word that the ancient Greek version of the Old Testament, the Septuagint, uses in chapter 2 of Genesis for God's seventh-day rest. In other words, the very first rest recorded in the story of the Bible, shortly after the world's foundation was

23 Hebrews 4:3–4.

laid, provides the essential foundation for understanding the final rest that God has planned for this world. The rest that lies ahead for all of God's people who believe his promises is in full continuity with God's rest when he celebrated the spectacular work he had wrought over the course of six creative days.

The text of Hebrews 4 operates, then, with three distinct "rests" and perhaps a fourth as well. There is the rest of God on the first seventh day, the rest of Canaan that a generation of Israel was denied, and there is the eternal rest celebrated on the day of resurrection. That the chapter seems at times to speak of believers entering rest already in the present could be read as a fourth sort of rest, a reference to justification by grace through faith apart from works. This possible fourth sense could seem to be at work in verses 3 and 10, where rest might be understood as something we have even now as we live freed from the burden of achieving salvation by our own efforts at keeping the law. No doubt, Christians certainly are able to delight and rest in God's grace in the present, yet we know the great and final rest still lies ahead. And it is also certainly possible simply to read these references to "the one who has entered His rest" as anticipatory or hypothetical and so still aimed at the final rest of the parousia. Perhaps the wise course is to see the rest we have in Christ, which is the subject of Hebrews 4, in light of the standard "now/not yet" tension that animates our life in the gospel. Right now we have Jesus' victory over sin, but we are not yet freed entirely from our struggle with sin; we have eternal life even now, but we have not yet overcome all suffering and physical death; right now we have rest in God's grace, but we still must strive against our own flesh to ensure that we do not "run in vain" or make "shipwreck in regard to [our] faith."[24] We celebrate sabbath in

24 Philippians 2:16; 1 Timothy 1:19.

our lives *now*, but the ultimate sabbath is still a *not yet* hope that will be ours fully only when Christ calls us up out of the grave into the unending celebration of his eternal kingdom.

While there is likely some intentional ambiguity at work in Hebrews 4 as the great Spirit-inspired gospel interpreter of the Old Testament teaches us about our rest in Christ, which begins now but is not yet fully realized, there should be no doubt that the final eschatological rest is paramount in his argument. Obviously, this rest still lies ahead. This is the "Sabbath rest" that "remains . . . for the people of God."[25] It is fascinating that this is the first and only direct use of the word *sabbath* in the entire book of Hebrews. That the writer invokes the word here is significant, and he does so with flair. In Greek, "Sabbath rest" is actually a single word, a word that in the entire biblical canon appears only here. It is as if the author of Hebrews coined the word to capture all the meaning that he wanted to load into the idea of the rest that continues to lie ahead for God's people, for you and for me—a rest that is in full continuity with, but greater by far than, all that went before. Our pending sabbath, the one we taste even now in the wonder of the gospel, is similar to, but infinitely more than, the weekly sabbaths that had shaped the people of Israel. It is even greater than the rest of the Promised Land. Our sabbath rest is the rest of the perfect celebration of God's perfect work of creation, perfectly restored once again through his Son's perfect work of redemption. This is the fullness and perfection of biblical rest that was established by the Father's work at creation, restored and heightened in Christ's work of redemption, and now lies ahead for all of us who believe and who cannot wait to witness the Spirit's work of consummation. This is the rest that grounds, animates, and fulfills the

25 Hebrews 4:9.

sabbath: the Father's seventh-day rest, Jesus' restoration, and the Spirit's final consummation.

After this selective foray into some key parts of the scriptural record, it should be clear that the Lord's rest, manifested in the sabbath, plays a critically important role within God's vastly sweeping yet meticulously intricate plan for his creation. God's rest was the guiding objective that drove his project of creation, which was realized and celebrated on day seven: the dynamic reality of his entire creation, capped with the crowning work of man and woman, all living and functioning exactly as he had designed. The rest that is sabbath is not a detour, a pit stop, or a reprieve from the busy-ness of life. Sabbath is not a necessary concession to ameliorate man's physical limitations. Sabbath rest is not a responsibility or a task to be fulfilled. God's rest observed in the establishment of the sabbath is the fullness of the rhythm of life in all of its complexity. It is the celebration of the Creator and every creature living in harmony according to God's plan. His master work begun and celebrated in Genesis will be perfected and exploded into exquisite full bloom at the eschatological fulfillment, when Christ returns to the world he redeemed. This is the fullness of sabbath rest.

r reason for we the
live the
Down & Out Life.

Delighting in the Down and Out Life

Day 7: Embracing God's Sabbath Gift
work, rest, or play
Re-thinking Sabbath

Joy fully living Down and Out
Life and the Joy

Brings

Sabbath and the Meaning of Existence

The Point of it All

God's Plan Gift Design for the Down and Out

Your Reason for Be

Sabbath Work: Re-Thinking God's Rest

God's Plan for

Receiving God's

CHAPTER 3

WORK

SITUATING OUR WORK

Work, for the vast majority of us, is the primary, defining, and norming activity of our adult lives. Most of our waking hours on most days are filled with work. Life revolves around work. And the work we need to do doesn't patiently wait for the arrival of adulthood or entirely cease with retirement. Besides the labor necessary for the sake of financial compensation, there are all the standard tasks of routine daily life that are required to keep our bodies fed, clothed, fit, and reasonably clean; our homes livable; our property protected and functioning as expected; and our dependents adequately sustained. Although we might quibble about what exactly qualifies as work or struggle precisely to define it (a solid definition is more elusive than it might seem), we all know the meaning and experience of work, and we all know that in our lives it is inescapable. We also know that there are probably few things that most people would consider to be less spiritual or linked to the practice of Christian faith than work. Work, especially the kind we do simply to meet the necessary demands of life, is the epitome of what is mundane, earthbound, and ordinary. There seems to be nothing even remotely ethereal, elevated, or spiritual about brushing teeth; dressing, feeding, and transporting kids; folding laundry; buying groceries; cleaning up after dinner; completing checklists; submitting reports; paying bills; or making customers happy. Even those whose work is compensated by the church may sometimes struggle to recognize in that work a direct and meaningful connection to the faith they profess or the relationship they have with their Creator. Like everyone else, their work is simply part of the routine of life. For all people, reality confronts us with things that need to be done, and so we do them. We work. There's nothing particularly spiritual, much less sacred, about any of it.

Such a stark assessment of the lack of spiritual or religious significance in our work will strike most readers as anything but insightful. Still the observation does challenge some familiar and widely held ideas that insist on a direct link between the motivational and inspirational power of Christian faith and the work required to sustain life in this world. Perhaps the most significant and enduring modern effort to identify such a connection was the idea known as the Protestant work ethic. It was first suggested and named by Max Weber in the early years of the twentieth century. The influential sociologist discerned a compelling correlation between the average American's professed Christian faith and the daily labor that occupied his life. Indeed, as the theory unfolds, Weber describes what seems to be a match made in heaven. The highly prized workplace virtues of diligence, discipline, and frugality are equally esteemed and encouraged among pious believers as just the sort of behavior one should expect from a faithful recipient of God's grace. Hard work was a tangible expression of what it meant to be a Christian believer. Calvinist and Puritanical traditions, in particular, with their emphasis on the importance of personal piety, good works, and general sanctification as confirmatory evidence of one's divine election provided an especially powerful bond between faith and work. Whether or not everyone embraced or even understood the theological underpinnings, the influence of this work ethic could be detected from America's earliest puritanical beginnings until it became a pervading feature of American culture at the outset of the 1900s. This characteristic work ethic inspired homey axioms for the conduct of life, and the truths were introduced and impressed on children as essential lessons in their elementary education: "work before play"; "be it big or be it small, do it well or not at all"; and "hard work never killed anyone." The defining message was powerful and pervasive: work mattered, and most of the time it mattered more than anything else.

As the twentieth century progressed and the theological component of the American work ethic collapsed, the cultural commitment to work nevertheless remained undiminished. In fact, it achieved stereotypical status. It was a fact taken for granted: America was a society committed to total work. Around the globe, Americans enjoy, or perhaps endure, the notorious reputation of people consumed by work, unable to take vacations, and obsessed with being productive. Anyone living in the United States has firsthand experience with the addiction. Activity that does not yield profit is deemed frivolous and a waste of time—unless it serves the tangential purpose of increasing later productivity. Unpacking the reasons for this preoccupation with one's occupation would be the project of an entire book in its own right, but a few observations can perhaps shed a little light. As Weber noted, from the time of the first European settlers in the New World, there was a strong spiritual or religious component to work. Hard work was the right thing to do. Productive work was a measure of personal worth and a source of affirmation and pride in doing the right thing for the right reasons: gratitude for God's grace, and earthly service and sacrifice in anticipation of heavenly joy and eternal blessing.

Work as the principal means of ensuring personal value and importance became embedded in the culture and continued even as the influence of religion, including generic American Protestantism, waned. By the latter years of the twentieth century, instead of work growing out of one's piety—a sign of salvation—it grew out of one's need for meaning and purpose in life. The sociologist and ardent cultural critic Philip Rieff called this the shift from "spiritual man" to "economic man." As Rieff saw it, spiritual man was born to be saved, but economic man was born to be productive in the workplace. However it was named or described, by the turn of the millennium, the average American worker was no longer driven by spiritual or religious motives but by the pure pragmatism of being productive in order to account for his own existence. Success gained through hard work confirmed personal significance and worth. In a world that had forsaken the meaning and purpose once supplied by the church, work was now used to provide life with meaning. But Rieff observed yet another shift in the temper of American culture. As the twentieth century progressed, economic man was being displaced by a phenomenon he called "psychological man." As Rieff memorably put it, if religious man was born to be saved, and economic man was born to produce, "psychological man is born to be pleased."[1] Rieff identified this shift already in the 1960s and labeled this cultural mindset "the therapeutic." In the world of the therapeutic, "to be entertained would become the highest good and boredom the most common evil."[2] Focused on maximizing personal pleasure and enhancing the enjoyable things in life, people living in the therapeutic-oriented world look at work as nothing more than a means to an end. Work provides the resources necessary to fund the real goal which is for people "to live their lives with a minimum of pretense to anything more grand than sweetening the time."[3]

Rieff's observations lend helpful perspective on one outcome of the coronavirus pandemic, which engulfed the world in 2020, that seems to have surprised many observers. Sobered,

1 Philip Rieff, *The Triumph of the Therapeutic: Uses of Faith after Freud* (Chicago: University of Chicago Press, 1966), 25.

2 Ibid., 5.

3 Ibid., 22.

perhaps, by hard lessons on the brevity of life or perhaps, less profoundly, motivated by the forced discovery of the sheer delight of days spent without having to work, many Americans, it has been widely reported, are no longer interested in working any more than absolutely necessary—and they have even less enthusiasm for jobs that demand the investment of their lives. This is precisely what one would expect of psychological man who is living in the world of the therapeutic, in which making life comfortable and pleasant is the thing that counts. Concurrent with this idea of the therapeutic but leading in an array of divergent, individualistic directions, one could add the burgeoning industry of personal entertainment streamed onto ever-expanding video screens, the destigmatizing and celebration of pornography, the normalization of deviant sexual expression, the expansion and mainstreaming of gambling, and the proliferation of legalized cannabis. But for this chapter and this book, we'll limit the consideration of the impact of the therapeutic on how we think about work and the place it occupies in our lives. The day when it was assumed that hard work done first and done well was a laudable life principle seems to have faded; and while Weber's old thesis might still be true, the application to the present American context seems much less apropos than it was 120 years ago. Perhaps the problem is that the premise no longer holds and there simply aren't enough ardent Protestants filling the land.

WORK CATEGORIZED

Things that are simply part of ordinary life typically occupy much of our effort and energy while paradoxically benefiting from very little direct reflection or careful thought about the thing itself. In other words, while we all think a great deal about work every day—from preparing for the next meeting to calculating whether there will be time to do a load of laundry before bedtime—we don't often think about the nature, meaning, or significance of work itself. Perhaps, as Aristotle would have thought, we are so busy trying to get our work done that we don't take time to ponder the very idea of work itself. People are sometimes surprised to learn that an entire field of extensive thought and research is dedicated to the idea of work itself. Yet, as this brief discussion about the role of work in the American mind and culture has indicated, work as an object to be studied and considered is a bit more complicated than most of us realize. Another safe conclusion arising from this cursory glance at the place of work in the American context is that we are living today in a transitional time in which many divergent assessments and understandings of work are present and accepted all at once.

I won't try my reader's patience with a deep dive into the various theories and understandings of work that occupy the worlds of philosophy, sociology, history, economics, and beyond. For my present purpose, it is sufficient to consider a theological understanding of work or, more specifically, a Christian understanding of work. To help set the stage for that particular exploration, it will be worthwhile to offer a brief overview of a few of the different ways that work may be broadly and generally understood. Gilbert Meilaender's engaging anthology *Working: Its Meaning and Its Limits* serves as a reliable guide for this endeavor. Meilaender organizes his selection of relevant material under four categories or headings that while "touching each other at points . . . are nonetheless different and distinct."[4] In his first grouping, work as co-creation, Meilaender includes the most idealized and even romantic ideas about work: those who

4 Gilbert Meilaender, *Working: Its Meaning and Its Limits* (University of Notre Dame, 2000), 1.

think about work as an extension of God's activity in the world and consider their work to be in some sense related to the divine work of God himself. Selections in this first category exude a strong affirmation of the nobility, joy, and perhaps even holiness of work in itself. Those who see work as a source of personal fulfillment, meaning, and satisfaction in life all fall within this category even if they aren't conscious of a spiritual component to their work, but it includes especially those who see themselves as mini creators in some sense like God the Creator.

To understand and appreciate the second of Meilaender's four groupings, work as necessary for leisure, I need to get ahead of myself just a bit and offer an advance introduction to the idea of leisure. Thinking about work as necessary for leisure is not the equivalent of "working for the weekend." In Meilaender's category, leisure is rightly being used in its classic sense as affording the time for reflection on and contemplation of life's most important questions and truths. This is the way that Josef Pieper uses the word in the title of his important book *Leisure: The Basis of Culture*, but that is the topic of the next chapter. For the ancients, like Aristotle, being able to think about the great truths of the world was the highest activity available to man and the most human of human activities, but one could only do this if time was available for this activity called leisure. In this context, work was considered as merely a servile activity that curtailed the possibility of leisure. The very best one could say about work was that it made possible times of leisure, that is, times for thinking and conversing about things that mattered. Clearly, this take on work is decidedly less favorable toward work than that of the first category.

The third grouping of readings represents an even bleaker perspective on work. Work as "dignified but irksome"[5]

5 Ibid., 69.

appreciates with almost a sense of awe the worth and honor attached to the workers who labor in difficult, unappreciated, and poorly compensated jobs, but exposes the hard truth that work is not always the source of personal fulfillment and meaning. Instead, work, as it is seen from the perspective of this category, methodically and mercilessly crushes both the body and soul of the worker. Coal miners bent double while tunneling deep in the crust of the earth or factory workers mindlessly repeating, several times each minute, a process both precise but incomprehensibly and impossibly linked in any obvious way to a final product, capture well the hard reality that for many people work is far from rewarding or magnifying and cannot possibly be construed as pleasurable—except perhaps when concluded.

Meilaender's final category, work as vocation, points back in a direction that seeks to affirm work, yet with the sober recognition that the work itself may demand and extract much from the worker. Categorizing work as vocation once again accents a divine aspect, as human work is esteemed as a responsibility given by God and carried out in accord with God's will. For Lutherans, this approach is comfortably familiar, as it was Luther who reclaimed the holiness of ordinary work for ordinary people at a time when the church had reserved a spiritual component of work only for those distinctly religious activities done in and for the church as priests, monks, or nuns. Luther exploded this notion and reshaped all of society by elevating the work of common life to a status even higher than that of those doing their work in the confines of a cloister. He argued that the young girl milking the cow was doing faithfully what God had given her to do, while the nun in the convent was actually neglecting her vocation and busy with work that had its origins only in the imagination of human creatures hoping to gain spiritual status or reward. Work as vocation may seem like the one best answer to the question of how we should think about our work—it does after all, come last in the list—but the reality is that even this idea has had its detractors who impugn the teaching as being static, confining, and dismissive of individual talents and interests. We'll come back to the vocational idea of work before we finish the chapter. For now, as we wrap up Meilaender's four groupings, it is enough to recognize that when careful attention is actually given to the idea of work, the entire topic quickly becomes at once very complicated and wonderfully interesting. But, before picking our way through the complexity to a solid, faithful, and rewarding understanding of work, one more wrinkle needs to be added.

Given the standard bullet-point list of things they have been taught about communism, most Christians will likely be surprised to learn that in his first grouping of thinkers, those who see work as co-creation, Meilaender includes Karl Marx. While the atheist Marx hardly seems a likely candidate for the category that also includes ardent Christian believers, Meilaender is right to do this. Marx actually held an exalted view of work and its singular importance for human identity and flourishing; and he dreamed of a paradisical, indeed, he would even say utopian, day when all people would be free to pursue their work readily and enthusiastically without compulsion and, perhaps as importantly, without alienation. One of his more particular and enduring contributions to the discussion of work is Marx's term "alienated work." This phrase has now taken on an almost technical meaning, but for Marx it aptly described the sorry plight of the proletariat who expended their labor for the benefit of others. Invariably underpaid and unappreciated, these laborers did hard, menial, mindless, and arguably dehumanizing work that was so far removed from an end product or the enjoyment of any of the profit that it was categorically impossible that their work ever could be considered to be personally significant, satisfying, or meaningful. On this topic, Marx's observations and criticisms actually echo concerns that readily resonate among Christians concerned for the right treatment of fellow creatures. It's also worth noting that the infamous father of atheistic communism fully endorses another distinctly Christian idea as he pines for that infamous utopian brotherhood of equals giving of themselves freely for the sake of the well-being of all—a final, fulfilling goal for the world that reflects, albeit dimly, the Christian hope of new heavens and new earth when Christ returns and makes all things new. Marx proves to be a fascinating and valuable voice for learning to think rightly about work.

THE PROBLEM AND ENIGMA OF WORK

The more thought we give to the common and utterly ordinary activity we call work, the more complicated this simple fact of life becomes. Is work a source of meaning? Does it belong to the essential definition of what it is to be human? Or is work at best a toilsome imposition on free creatures? Is it nothing but an unfortunately necessary burden to be endured only to the extent required to sustain more interesting and humane pursuits? Is work a gift or a curse? And, specifically and importantly in the context of this book's focus on sabbath, is it possible to conceive of work as anything other than the polar opposite of sabbath rest? Given the biblical articulation of Israel's specific sabbath laws in terms of the prohibition of all work, it seems that there is little prospect for human work to be considered as anything more than the antithesis of sabbath itself. Granting that the evidence seems to be stacked against me, I am nevertheless going to make the case that work and sabbath are not only *not* antithetical but are actually dynamically and essentially related. Indeed, I believe it is absolutely possible to provide answers to all the questions leveled in this paragraph and demonstrate that these are definitely not mere rhetorical questions incapable of being answered. I'll tackle the easiest one first, the penultimate, or second-to-last, question in the list: Is work a gift or a curse? Once again, turning to the creation account yields enormous dividends both in answers and in our understanding.

Read Genesis 1 and the answer is unequivocal: work is, at the very least, a gift given to Adam. Indeed, work is revealed as Adam's *raison d'être*, his reason for being. The man is created to tend the creation God had only recently called into existence. "Be fruitful and multiply, and fill the earth, and subdue it; and rule over the fish of the sea and over the birds of the sky and over every living thing that moves on the earth."[6] Thus, Adam exists in and for the creation. He is there to rule—or more specifically, to serve as steward or caretaker over God's great work. Genesis 2 reiterates and confirms man's place in creation: "Then the LORD God took the man and put him into the garden of Eden to cultivate it and keep it."[7] Tending the creation means doing work; it is the only way to discharge the required duties. In the creation accounts, the truth is simple and straightforward: Adam was created to work. Once this fact has been established, all the other questions are readily resolved in quick succession. Work is certainly a gift. It is enormously meaningful. It is, in fact, an essential aspect of what it means to be human. In this light, work cannot be considered an imposition or burden on mankind but only a beneficent action and gift of God on behalf of human creatures.

6 Genesis 1:28.
7 Genesis 2:15.

Genesis 3 recounts the tragic story of man's rejection of God's plan. In light of man's sin and creation's fall, the rest of the complicated picture of human work in our world today comes into sharp focus. After calling to account each of his rebellious creatures in turn—Adam, then Eve, and finally the serpent—God then pronounces his curse and judgment in ascending order of responsibility: the serpent, Eve, and finally Adam as the one creature specifically accountable for the whole of creation. Each curse is specific to each creature. The snake who exalted himself now crawls on his belly and eats dust, the woman who carries forward the gift of life endures pain in childbirth and now finds her place in the creational order onerous, and Adam is compelled to strive against the newly hostile, fallen creation he had been created to steward. What had been Adam's very reason for being is now the locus of his sharpest suffering. His work hurts. It wears him down. It kills him. His work has become a burden birthed by the curse. Given the brokenness of the creation—a brokenness inflicted on the creation by the custodian of creation himself—work can only be precisely the conflicted, complicated, and contradictory reality each man experiences firsthand in his own life each day. He is drawn to work and finds purpose and significance in his work, and yet he languishes in his work, is ground down by it, and resents it. Work is at once a gift and blessing and an affliction and burden.

While the oppositional and paradoxical nature of human work is the reality in which we find ourselves at present, it must be remembered that this is not the inherent or defining nature of work itself. Rather, it is only the sorry consequence of man's sin and the tragedy of a cursed creation. In other words, what we know of life as we now encounter it, including our contradictory ideas and experiences related to the work we do, is not the reality God intended and it is not the inherent truth about creaturely existence. The truth about our lives is what Jesus declared and accomplished—a truth that overcomes the horrible repercussions of sin and reclaims all of creation for the Father, restoring the entire creation back to the Father's intent. This means that within God's plan, work is not eradicated in the new creation but is actually reestablished as it was always supposed to be, at the center of man's very reason for existence.

The implications of this understanding of work are enormous and significant. This means that man does not work as a punishment. Work itself is not part of the curse. And it also means that work cannot be reduced to the status of a secondary, supporting role for something more essential to our human being. In other words, the idea that one works only to the degree necessary to pursue leisure is fundamentally wrong about what it means to be human—though as we'll see in the next chapter, one cannot simply dispense with or reject the equally important insight that a human life certainly is about more than *just* work. For now, though, it is enough for us to appreciate human work as a fundamental, defining part of human existence and not an unwelcome imposition on our living or our being. In this regard, it bears remembering that the reason human work is so often irksome or even alienating is not a fault inherent in work itself but only a bitter consequence of living in a fallen world shot through with sin and its devastation.

If we rightly understand work as a necessary component of what it means to be human, we can also avoid the mistake of thinking of work as somehow antithetical to sabbath. Indeed, if we are able to grasp both work and sabbath rightly, we will recognize that work is not only compatible with sabbath but actually an integral aspect of sabbath as intended by the Creator. Of course, the weekly moratorium on all work whether by man or beast is unequivocally declared in the Pentateuch. But as noted in the previous chapter, this prohibition on work can readily and rightly be understood as simply the specific rules for, or outward manifestation of, Israel's practice and not the heart of the sabbath commandment itself. And it is good to recall that in a fallen world where the central and defining task of work has also fallen under God's curse, a day without work is a welcome reminder of still greater truths that have been built into the creation. Yet, if we are content to understand sabbath as basically a ban on work and establish an inherent opposition between work and sabbath, we are missing the point of both. Instead, when we think about sabbath in a more complete and foundational way, not as a bare proscription of work but as the celebration of Creator and creation delighting together in the wonder and beauty of the Creator's masterpiece as we established in the previous chapter, we are able to see work as a vital part of the creation and as one of the reasons for the sabbath celebration. This is to say that work is not the opposite of sabbath or even the flip side of sabbath. Instead, work is a part of sabbath, an essential component of a creation functioning as intended. This reveling and delight in the wonders of God's creation is the very focus and impetus for the festival created by God on the world's first seventh day, the festival that would come to define life for God's people and eventually be called sabbath.

THE ESSENTIAL REALITY OF WORK

All of this means that work is not incidental to our human existence, but an essential part of it. To put it even more strongly, work is part of what it means to be human. In a thorough and engaging study on the topic of work, Darrell Cosden convincingly argues that work must be "viewed as fundamentally a part of what it means to be a human being."[8] He contends that work is not simply an instrumental part of life necessary for survival, or even a tool for spiritual accomplishments. "Rather," he concludes, "it is a fundamental condition of human created existence. It is ontological."[9] The last sentence is deliberately loaded and every bit as profound as it sounds. To claim that work is an ontological part of our human being is to assert that work is part of what makes us what we are. It is tied to the very core of our being as humans. Work is not an add-on or an embellishment of our humanity but is a necessary part of what it means to be human. The argument is that we are literally built to work. Though it may seem an extraordinary claim, I don't believe that Cosden is overstating his case. The creation account supports his case. And so does the reality of human experience.

We have all experienced the tug to "do something" and the lure to be productive and useful. No doubt, we have all also felt the pull to listlessness and lethargy and know well the temptation to do nothing and accomplish even less. Sin's reach extends to the very core of our being and seeks to thwart or pervert even the work for which we were created—and often succeeds. And yet, the deep-seated urge to accomplish something of worth, to be of benefit in some way, to tackle some project, and to do useful work remains a part of us and routinely surfaces and asserts itself—sometimes in spite of our best efforts to ignore or suppress it. And even when God's plan does not prevail in our lives, even when the evidence of work's ontological status in our human being is meager or all but nonexistent, even

8 Darrell Cosden, *A Theology of Work: Work and the New Creation* (Eugene, OR: Wipf & Stock, 2004), 144. Used by permission of Wipf and Stock Publishers, www.wipfandstock.com.

9 Ibid.

when we wantonly fritter and waste the hours and days in fruitless idleness, the truth remains unchanged. It is wired into the very structure of creation: God has designed us to work. It's part of our very being. And when our sinful selves do subvert this natural law established by God, he extends grace yet again, and led by his Spirit, we confess both our sin and the truth of God's plan and embrace once more the reality of what it means to be human the way God intended us to be—doing work for the sake of his world.

Sin seriously challenges our ability to see work as a gift from God to lend purpose, fulfillment, and significance to our lives. And since sin is an inescapable part of our lives, coloring and distorting how we see everything including our work, it can be helpful and perhaps encouraging to remember that God created his world free from sin and its curse, and the work that defined Adam's existence was altogether unlike our own experience of working "by the sweat of our face." Luther once observed, "For Adam [work] would have been supreme joy, more welcome than any leisure."[10] Indeed. This is yet another simple but pithy statement freighted with deep significance. Here, Luther declares that work is so central to Adam's reason for being that doing the work he has been given to do provides him with the greatest possible joy—greater even than the joy of leisure. Luther's comment is a remarkable but true claim and one that will gain even more significance when understood in light of the next chapter's excursion into the depth of meaning connected to leisure.

We may not be able to enjoy now the unbridled delight in our work the way that Adam would have enjoyed his work in Eden. But someday we will. And in the meantime, as we live in the restoration brought through the redeeming work of Christ, we can

10 Martin Luther, *Luther's Works*, vol. 1, *Lectures on Genesis*, ed. Jaroslav Pelikan (St. Louis: Concordia Publishing House, 1958), 82.

sample a foretaste of the fullness of Christ's coming kingdom. We learn to see our work in our many vocations as tasks given to us by God and done as his creatures in service to the rest of his creation. Unpacking that idea a bit more will be the task of the remainder of the chapter. But before embarking on that, it's worth noting explicitly what has been repeatedly suggested: that understanding our work in an ontological way, as part of our very being as humans, not only has implications for our lives today as it puts work into rather a different light but also has profound implications for the life we will celebrate with our Lord upon his return on the Last Day. Fully renewed and at last all that God always intended us to be, complete with resurrected and perfected bodies, we will step into God's new heavens and new earth and do there what God created us to do. We will work. Granted, this idea may seem incongruous with the imagery most people tend to conjure when they reflect on the glories of heaven or, stated more precisely, the glories of the consummation of God's plan for his creation at the return of Christ, when all things are made new. But when seen in the context of the full biblical picture, there is good reason to believe that Christ's kingdom in all of its fullness has less in common with an eternal church service than it does with life in Eden, complete with celebrating, eating, and working.

Still, it is true that we won't know exactly what details and realities will comprise the coming glories of God's restoration of his creation. The often heavily symbolic and suggestive picture given in the pages of the Bible, especially in the Apocalypse of St. John, does plenty to fire the imagination. Duly inspired, Christian popular piety has never demonstrated much hesitation or restraint when it comes to speculating about the life to come. The results of such speculation often take root in the convictions of Christians and sometimes even supplant or distort clear scriptural truths that are revealed. But to suggest work as part of the new world to come is not merely speculation. It is not speculation when St. Paul declares that we will each be raised as the individual human beings God created us each to be.[11] And it is not speculation to declare that we will be fully human at the resurrection with unique souls and bodies together as God always planned humans to be. Neither is it speculation to offer the idea that a restored human being will be doing what God created humans to do: looking after his creation.

Each reader can flesh out the details of that picture according to the sort of creational work that suits the sort of person he or she has been formed to be. To offer any more detail *would* be pure speculation—though I will admit that through the years I've been known to suggest that my own view of an eternal job description might well involve a generous swath of bluegrass so thick it feels like a sponge under your feet and a freshly tuned and sharpened lawn mower. There is something profoundly satisfying about perfectly parallel stripes reaching from corner to corner across a lush lawn fairly dripping the pungent fragrance of fresh-cut spring grass. Idle and groundless conjecture? I think not. I am convinced that the burden of proof lies with those who insist on a glittering, work-free heaven. Why would we expect fully redeemed and restored human beings to do anything other than what God created them to do in the first place? What better way is there to honor and praise God than to do what he wants us to do? No doubt, we can be quite certain that the work that will occupy us in the eternal kingdom will be, as Luther was sure it once was for Adam (for however long he and Eve reveled in their Edenic lives), sheer delight with more joy than any leisure.[12]

11 See 1 Corinthians 15:42–54.

12 Despite its problematic intimations toward purgatory, J. R. R. Tolkien's short story "Leaf by Niggle" wonderfully captures this reality.

LUTHER'S OTHER BREAKTHROUGH

Every Protestant knows that Martin Luther's great gift to the church was his "discovery" of the gospel. Of course, he didn't actually discover it. Luther himself would be the first to insist that God's gospel found him. Exhausted and desperate in his efforts to gain assurance of God's approval, Martin threw himself unreservedly into the church's prescribed path to heavenly security and eternal bliss. He became an exemplary monk. But that path did not provide the one thing Luther yearned to find. He had no peace; his own sin and failure relentlessly harassed and condemned and kept any glimmer of joy or rest far from the tortured young monk. And then God's grace found him, and from that moment nothing was ever the same. While Luther crafted lectures on Romans, the Holy Spirit crafted Luther and led him to realize that God's righteousness was not the exacting goal that he had to achieve but was, in fact, the gift of God, freely offered and profusely given to him through the life, death, and resurrection of God's own Son, Jesus Christ. Luther's clear recognition of the gospel heart of Christianity changed everything for him—and eventually for the world. For those who study Luther and his teaching, this singular change is known simply as Luther's breakthrough.

Related to the gospel breakthrough—in fact, happening at nearly the same time—and arguably equally impactful yet much less familiar is Luther's other great breakthrough: Luther's realization that what God desires from his creatures is not a life devoted to a single-minded, all-consuming pursuit of spiritual perfection aimed at eternal salvation and union with God, but a life spent in sacrificial service to other creatures here in this world. To be sure, such a life was possible only because union with God and spiritual perfection were already accomplished facts. Righteousness before God was not a mountain to summit nor a trophy to be won but a generous gift already given in the gospel. This meant that a life rightly lived was not consumed with scrupulous attention to prayer, worship, fasting, killing the flesh, and forsaking the world in the hope of one day being worthy of God. That worthiness was already granted in Christ. Luther came to realize, then, that a life rightly lived was one immersed in fulfilling the demands and realities imposed by the material world surrounding the redeemed Christian believer right now. Being human as God intended was not defined by an escape from the world and the work of earthbound creatures. Humans made righteous in Christ, and so newly shaped and at last rightly aimed, were intent on fulfilling their responsibilities, duties, and tasks in the creation for the sake of fellow creatures. In short, Luther's other breakthrough was his discovery of vocation.

For too long, Luther's other breakthrough was neglected, tucked away in forgotten, untranslated, and unappreciated treatises in Fraktur text, bound in worm-eaten volumes and shelved in a long row of "Luther's Works" in a dusty corner of a deserted library. To the great benefit of the church, this began to change in the twentieth century with what has come to be known as the Luther Renaissance. The rediscovery of Luther's work and fresh enthusiasm for his keen doctrinal thought has continued apace ever since. It was the Swedish theologian Gustaf Wingren, in particular, who propelled Luther's teaching about vocation back into the thinking and conversations of the heirs of the Reformation, including me. Wingren scoured his Luther sources and brought together the reformer's thinking about the twofold dynamic that norms the life of every human. In our relationship with God, we receive what God gives; and in our relationships with other creatures, we give of ourselves for the benefit of our neighbors. Using the idea of conscience to designate man in his vertical relationship with God and referring to man's hands to account for the horizontal relationship, Wingren makes the distinction clear: "Conscience rests in faith in God, and does nothing that contributes to salvation; but the hands serve in the vocation which is God's downward-reaching work, for the well-being of men."[13]

Vocation is not an unfamiliar word to us. We hear about people pursuing this or that vocation from the noteworthy to the mundane, or perhaps choosing to study at a vocational school rather than doing more academic work at a university. In our twenty-first-century context, vocation is typically associated with occupation or career, or what one does to make a living. In popular thought, you leave home to go somewhere else to do your vocation; a person "goes to work" is the way we usually put it. But a person's job or profession done for compensation is not the best point of departure for a right understanding of vocation. Vocation is grounded in the home, in the family, in relationships. Vocation begins before birth. Vocation is not selected. It is given.

Like so much of our English vocabulary, the word *vocation* comes from a Latin root: *vocare* is the Latin verb "to call." As in English, the verb form easily morphs into a noun form—in this case, a calling. The basic idea, then, is that vocation is something one is called into, or called to do. In the context of Christian faith, it is helpful to think about vocation in the context of the two fundamental relationships that define every human life: our relationship with the Creator and our relationships with fellow creatures. In the vertical relationship between creature and God, the initiative and action belong entirely

13 Gustaf Wingren, *Luther on Vocation*, reprint ed. (Eugene, OR: Wipf & Stock, 2004), 11. Used by permission of Wipf and Stock Publishers, www.wipfandstock.com.

to God. He calls a person to faith, and he gives the gift of the gospel. We creatures simply receive. We can say, then, that God calls us into faith, into the kingdom of heaven, into the community of the church, and into an unfailing hope. This calling or vocation in the vertical realm is common to every believer and establishes our status as God's children for eternity.[14] This use of the word *vocation*, however, is not what is in mind when we talk about Luther's other breakthrough, or his teaching of vocation. Luther's use of the word *vocation* centers on life in this world and our relationships with other creatures. As Wingren puts it, "So vocation belongs to this world, not to heaven; it is directed toward one's neighbor, not toward God."[15]

In the horizontal sphere of our lives, in all the relationships and responsibilities that constitute our creaturely existence in this world, vocation is the name for the particular tasks and activities that attend each of these relationships and responsibilities. Our earthly relationships are established from the time we come into existence at the moment of conception. As Christians we know and gladly confess that once again it is God who is solely at work establishing the truths of these callings. He determined where and when you would be born and to which set of parents. It was his plan that established your first and most significant vocations. You were son or daughter and perhaps sibling along with a host of other family roles—and you did not choose any of it. The choice to marry, have children, create friendships, enter the workforce, and perhaps pursue a hobby or two created a wealth of further relationships. Along with each new relationship came another set of obligations or responsibilities. Each of these unique relationships can rightly be named a vocation—a

14 This is the sense of "calling" that St. Paul uses in places like 1 Corinthians 1:26 and Romans 11:29.

15 Wingren, 10.

calling, ultimately from God, to serve another creature with some peculiar set of duties or commitments.[16] In the horizontal realm, vocation begins and imposes its greatest expectations and demands at home. So, a person does not leave home to do his vocation or say goodbye to his family before he "goes to work." Vocation and work are both centered in and orbit around the home and the defining relationships grounded there and then expand outward into every place where the life of the Christian intersects with others in the world.

VOCATION AS THE KEY TO WORK

Seen this way, it becomes evident that every Christian operates within an array of vocations. Throughout our lives, new vocations begin and others come to an end, corresponding with the beginning and ending of different relationships. Even the vocations that endure throughout an entire life rarely stay exactly the same; the responsibility of a son to his father is quite different at age 1, 13, 24, or 62, and yet all of those vastly different tasks are circumscribed beneath the umbrella of the single vocation of son. There is, then, a dynamic aspect inherent in the very idea of calling. Oddly enough, however, one of the perennial criticisms leveled against a Lutheran doctrine of vocation is that it is thought to be too static, restrictive, stagnating, and unresponsive. Vocation is sometimes dismissed as overly conservative and incapable of useful application in the modern world. Since there is an undeniable aspect of continuity and longevity involved especially in familial vocations, it is certainly possible that vocation could be invoked to "keep people in their place." There is, however, nothing calcifying or stultifying that is inherent in the teaching. In fact, unresponsiveness and

16 This is the way the apostle Paul uses the word in 1 Corinthians 7:17–24.

resistance to change should be seen as aberrations or denials of a correct and faithful teaching of vocation. When one is paying attention to what other creatures need from him, he will be compelled to think continually about what exactly is required of him or the best form of service in any given situation.

The vocations that grow out of our connections to family and friends are anything but static—though they may very well be quite demanding and at times even overwhelming. There is no guarantee that every or even any vocation will be easily done or readily accomplished. Nevertheless, every vocation given by God by virtue of our relationships is without question a significant source of the work that we do in our lives as humans—work that is an essential part of what it means to be human. Given that peculiar individual identities of each one of God's people extend through death and are brought to the fullness of God's plan on the day of Christ's triumphant return, it does not seem much of a stretch to suggest that even in the age to come humans will continue to serve each other in the context of the unique relationships that bind them to one another. In other words, perhaps at the resurrection we will still be called to particular areas of work that benefit other creatures, much as Adam was called to precisely such service in the garden, where God had placed him and called him to work.

It should be clear that the vocations we have each been given as human creatures are not limited to spiritual pursuits—in fact, in light of Luther's other breakthrough, vocations that are truly God-directed and God-pleasing should be understood as antithetical to a monastic life of seclusion from the world and a renunciation of creaturely connections. To fully appreciate this somewhat counterintuitive idea that rightly serving God actually means focusing not on heaven but on life in this world, it is worth hearing Luther at some length. He addressed this topic head-on in 1532 when preaching on Matthew 6.

> In the world's eyes it's a big deal when a monk denies himself everything, enters a cloister, leads a disciplined, austere life, fasts, prays, and so on. No lack of activity exists there, except only that God's command is lacking to do these things. Therefore, this cannot be extolled as serving God. On the other hand, when a maid cooks, washes, sweeps, and does other housework, it is looked down upon as trivial. But since there is a command from God for this, such trivial work cannot but be extolled as a service to God, surpassing by far all the holiness and austere life of all monks and nuns.[17]

This is the thinking behind Luther's beloved and frequently repeated claim that a young girl obediently milking a cow as directed by the lady of the household is doing a vocation far more pleasing to God than is an earnest monk zealously and devoutly pursuing the path of righteousness prescribed by his order. Luther's rationale is simple and correct: the girl is doing what God has called her to do. The monk is forsaking the honorable and useful worldly work God has called him to do and replacing it with exertions, chores, and rituals given not by God but conjured by man. As Luther himself summarizes: "Serving God means to do what God has commanded in his Word, each

17 Eugene F. A. Klug, ed., *Sermons of Martin Luther: The House Postils*, vol. 3 (Grand Rapids: Baker, 1996), 14.

person in his station and calling."[18] True vocations are always aimed at service within the creation for the benefit of other creatures. Most of the pursuits that occupy the attention of monks accomplish neither. Vocations, then, are certainly not limited to occupations or service in the church, though it should be noted that Roman Catholicism continues to use the word *vocation* in precisely this way. For Rome, an exhortation to "pray for vocations" is a prayer for priests and nuns. And while the church absolutely needs faithful servants, even the service of full-time church work is never aimed at God but aimed at serving the needs of the neighbor—specifically, the neighbor's crying need to hear a clear proclamation of God's truth and receive a certain delivery of the gospel. It is true of every vocation; it "belongs to this world, not to heaven, it is directed toward one's neighbor, not toward God." Because, after all, "God does not need our good works, but our neighbor does."[19]

Vocations are part of our lives as God's creatures who are living as integral parts of God's creation. It is in and through our various vocations that we do the work God has given us to do. It is in the vocations of home, extended family, church, school, friendship, employment, hobby, and society that we live appropriately worldly lives as the creatures God made us to be. In the context of the full range of our vocations, it is clear that many of our most foundational and perhaps most demanding vocations are those we did not choose, and yet it is also clear that some of our vocations are those that God calls us to enter willingly and deliberately so that we may be of service to those around us. This truth once again reinforces the variable and adaptable nature of vocations. God makes each of us unique individuals with vastly different personalities, talents, inclinations,

18 Ibid., 10.
19 Ibid.

aptitudes, skills, and abilities. In his vivid imagery of the church as a body, Paul makes explicit what we all know: we are not all alike or even interchangeable; we are not all identically crafted and gifted.[20] Jesus' parable of the talents highlights the same fact and reinforces the responsibility each of us has to use what we have been given to accomplish God's purpose.[21] And God's purpose, as we have seen, is that his creatures embrace their lives within his creation and serve the other creatures around them.

This means that each of us is accountable for our use of the gifts given to us, both the ordinary and the peculiar, by our Creator and Lord. Considering the distinctive gifts given to each of us leads us to recognize the malleable and nimble nature of a faithful teaching about vocations. As we each contemplate our unique giftedness, we are compelled into diametrically different and yet wonderfully complementary areas of work. So, the charge that vocation is somehow constraining is simply wrong. A boy born to a farmer certainly has vocational tasks as a son within that family; but that same child, along with his parents, is obligated also to discern and then use the particular talents and gifts bestowed on the boy by the Creator. Following that course could very well take him off the farm and land him in a university, a theater or musical group, a large corporation, or a medical research center. Luther already recognized this aspect of vocations done rightly as he admonished parents: "Therefore let all people know that it is their chief duty—at the risk of losing divine grace—first to bring up their children in the fear and knowledge of God, and then, if they are so gifted, also to have them engage in formal study and learn so that they may be of service wherever they are needed."[22] Through the manifold gifts

20 See 1 Corinthians 12.

21 See Matthew 25:14–30.

22 Large Catechism, Ten Commandments, paragraph 174.

he gives, God calls us each into unique places of service, even as he continues to call us to fulfill our responsibilities in those vocations given at birth. Sorting out the sometimes conflicting demands of all these vocations is the work of a lifetime and one best carried out within the community of the church, where each person can benefit from the accumulated wisdom of those around who are likewise engaged in the continuing challenge of learning how best to honor God by pouring oneself out in service to others.

CONCLUSION

In many ways, the doctrine of vocation is similar to the doctrine of election. Both are essential aspects of faithful Christian confession, and both spotlight the sovereign work of God, who arranges all things as he chooses. Both doctrines are further alike in that when they are rightly understood, taught, and practiced, they bring extraordinary comfort and assurance to God's people—and when they are misunderstood, twisted, or wrongly applied, they can generate a great deal of angst and confusion among God's people. Knowing that God has chosen for each of us our place in life and given us the special gifts we have in order to serve those around us liberates the Christian to throw herself headlong into that work, to shoulder the burdens that come, and to delight in the joys that also come when doing the vocations given by God. It is the same sort of liberating celebration that ensues when we realize that our eternal salvation is entirely the work of God, who simply chose us for his own and released us from all doubt and uncertainty about our standing before God. In both cases, we are freed from self-absorbed and self-defeating introspection and worry about who we are and what we are doing. We simply belong to God, and we are free to do whatever our hand finds to do as Solomon once wisely directed.[23] We are careful, then, not to obsess over our standing or place either before God or other creatures, forever wondering if we are doing everything "right." Such preoccupation with self is a fundamentally wrong use or application of both the doctrine of election as well as the doctrine of vocation. Such self-absorption can only end badly as those intent on securing their own standing in either sphere, whether in election or vocation, will spiral into the abyss of doubt and apprehension—the inevitable outcome when life is focused on self. The Christian life is built on the foundational truth that we are recipients. We receive what God gives—both the gospel gift of salvation along with the law-related gifts that shape and norm our lives in this world, gifts of meaningful purpose and direction for our lives among fellow creatures.

Work is not simple, nor is it hopelessly complicated. In spite of all the vagaries and difficulties that attend even a half-hearted examination of work, when seen in light of the Creator's plan for his creation, the place, importance, and right understanding of work for human life emerge in sharp outline. To work is to engage in effort and activity aimed at achieving some objective or accomplishing some productive end or goal. Work brings plans into existence. It makes ideas reality. Work gets things done. Humans are built to work. It is an essential aspect of our human being. God put us in the creation to work. To be human is to work. Work is not an optional component that a human creature can take or leave as he sees fit. Work is part of our human nature. And yet, work is not a tool a Christian can exploit or "leverage" for personal benefit. Work does not create my being or determine my identity or secure my image, whether

23 Ecclesiastes 9:10.

before man or God. I don't work for my own sake but for the sake of others. I work to serve the world, to get things done for the good of those around me.[24]

When rightly understood, the work we do in this world has at once everything to do with God . . . and nothing to do with God. Coming from God and directed by his will for the right functioning of creation as expressed in the Ten Commandments, our work is entirely established and directed by God, who determines everything about our core vocations. Our work is his idea, and we work because God himself has built us to work. And yet, when we are each busily doing what God has given us each to do, our eyes stop scanning the heavens for some object or beneficiary of our efforts and instead our vision settles on the world around us. Our attention is absorbed by the situations and needs of our fellow creatures, and our efforts are devoted to serving those around us. We are consumed not with pursuing God above but with addressing and alleviating the needs of fellow creatures here below. And we invest especially in caring for those near us, doing whatever we can to serve them by using the peculiar gifts given to each of us by God. The Creator gives us our work, but we do our work for the sake of fellow creatures.

We see, then, that a right understanding of work further erodes that old and familiar, but artificial and disastrous, false division between activities, events, and things that are considered to be sacred and activities, events, and things that are deemed merely secular. All work, even thoroughly secular or world-bound work, is God-pleasing and holy when done in obedience to God's will for the sake of the neighbor. And while we are busy doing our work for the sake of the neighbor here in this

24 These are important ideas that will be explored much more fully in chapter 5.

world, the gospel gifts of God's grace continually suffuse us and flow through us and out to others. Our inevitable shortcomings, inabilities, and failures to use rightly what we have been given to use, or to do well what we have been given to do, are all smothered beneath the overwhelming forgiveness of Christ. Thus, the most sacred spiritual truth of the gospel touches all of our life and work, forgiving us and then inviting those around us to see in and behind our worthy work not only a faithful creature but the generous and faithful Creator.

CHAPTER 4

LEISURE

MEETING PIEPER

Apparently the '70s are not cool—at least not as cool as the '80s. Several stations on my radio dial (an anachronistic term dying a slow but inevitable death) highlight playlists with "hits from the '80s and today." And my students revel in throwback parties that oblige people to "dress like the '80s." But I witness no such enthusiasm for the '70s. Perhaps the '70s deserve the snub, though I definitely don't concede the superiority of the '80s. Frankly, I don't harbor much nostalgia for any decade, not even for my own coming-of-age decade, the sorry '70s. Indeed, I am old enough that my high school years and that long, sad decade finished together. So I am credentialed; I can speak with authority about the cultural wasteland that was the late '70s, as well as the wasteland that was my public high school education at the close of that forgettable era. I was more than happy to see both come to an end. The noteworthy cultural events of my high school years were the Iran hostage crisis, the energy crisis, the affliction of disco, and the death of Elvis. The early part of the decade gave us Watergate, *Roe v. Wade*, the breakup of the Beatles, and Yoko singing with John. No doubt, there is much in the decade to lament and not much to fuel warm nostalgia or retroactive interest. Of all the horrors of the '70s, though, perhaps none can eclipse that of the leisure suit. With color palettes ranging from mint green to baby blue, bell-bottom pants, and expansive lapels overlayed with the enormous collars of garish nylon print shirts, the leisure suit epitomized the tired, tasteless kitsch of the disco culture of the '70s—a decade to forget, indeed. But there is so much that is so hard to forget, and for an eyewitness like me, the word *leisure* has been forever tainted.

So it was that when during my graduate studies I first encountered a footnote reference to Josef Pieper's book *Leisure:*

The Basis of Culture, my reaction was less than enthusiastic.[1] At best, it was perplexity bordering on suspicion. Confronted, however, with the strong affirmation with which the book was consistently referenced, I surmised that the title's apparent endorsement of leisure had to have been intended in a sarcastic or at least a provocatively ironic way. I was sure any claim that leisure—even a non-70s, benign sort of leisure—could be the basis of culture must be meant as an exasperated lament or withering accusation aimed at the self-indulgent culture of the modern West. When I secured my own copy and started to read Pieper's book, I ignorantly, well . . . ok, foolishly. . . waited expectantly for the German scholar to unleash a withering literary attack on the leisure-loving culture of the decadent West. That attack never came, but I was not disappointed in the least. Oddly enough, it turns out that actually reading the book disabused me of my errant assumptions. It is remarkable what actually reading a book can do to a person's presumptions about said book. Not only did Pieper's short book force me to rethink my understanding of leisure, but it also basically blew my mind. It still does. It ranks among the most influential books I've read. I wasn't expecting such an impact. Pieper took me entirely by surprise.

Part of the surprise likely stemmed from the fact that my training for the pastoral ministry relied heavily on the work of another Pieper whose reputation is secure in the world of conservative Lutheranism. Franz Pieper was the student of C. F. W. Walther and served as president of both the Missouri Synod and Concordia Seminary as the nineteenth century gave way to the twentieth. In my denomination, he is legendary. The three volumes of his *Christian Dogmatics* were the core texts of my

1 Josef Pieper, *Leisure: The Basis of Culture*, trans. Alexander Dru (San Francisco: Ignatius Press, 1952).

seminary systematics courses. Twenty years later, in my first years of teaching at the seminary, a century after Pieper's tenure, it was my turn to lead students through each volume of Pieper's magnum opus from cover to cover. From all that I had learned, I thought I knew what to expect from a Pieper. Other than their surname and German heritage, however, there is little that Josef Pieper shares with Franz. Josef Pieper was a Roman Catholic, Thomist philosopher, and moral theologian who lived a generation or two after Franz. Not only are the theological traditions and interests of each Pieper quite distinct, so is the writing style of each. Franz is utterly thorough, orderly, and careful; in a word, he is systematic. Josef is brief, almost terse, moves swiftly to make his points, and is content to allow a number of loose ends at the edge of his arguments that winsomely beckon further thought and speculation. Franz wants to settle all questions. Josef wants to inspire and multiply them. For very different reasons, I owe much to both Piepers, but it is the little book by Josef with his remarkable insights into the centrality of leisure for a life lived well that shapes this chapter's exploration.

COMING TO TERMS WITH LEISURE

By now, it should be clear that what Pieper and this chapter mean by *leisure* has essentially nothing at all to do with the '70s fashion disaster that was the leisure suit. Indeed, leisure as Pieper uses it in his title, which is the same understanding of leisure I will try to explain in this chapter, has very little in common with most of our usual ideas about leisure. Our present usage of leisure conjures images of a lazy afternoon slung in a hammock swaying in the sea breeze beneath the shade of spreading palms. Or we visualize the packed tables and bustling bar, driving music, shouted conversations, and general spirit of frivolity that defines Friday afternoon happy hour. Or leisure makes us think of a golf course still damp with dew; a mountain trail stretching out ahead; a tennis court, ball field, or soccer pitch; or just a theater-scale TV on which we can vicariously participate in whatever leisure activities we favor. English dictionaries will tell you that leisure is free time—or more precisely, the time when not working or doing other duties. While defining leisure in opposition to work does fall within the orbit of Pieper's usage, there is much more going on with Pieper's leisure than merely the absence of work.

Josef Pieper's assertion of leisure as foundational for society is not merely advocacy for a shorter work week, more vacation time, the pursuit of pleasant pastimes, or the cultivation of social activities meant to reward or restore those drained by hard work. Pieper is not suggesting that an ideal culture is one premised on the creation of idle time or the enhancement of amusements and distracting pleasures. The idea of leisure endorsed by Pieper does not include indulging bodily impulses, participating in frivolous games and activities, or even cultivating some interesting hobby for the sake of passing the time. No, the leisure of interest to Pieper and to me that lies at the center and bottom of culture is the sort that was identified by the ancient Greeks. They called it *skole*. In Latin it was called *schola*. Yes, this is the root for the English words *school* and *scholar*. Oddly enough, understood in its classic context, leisure shares more in common with a day in a school classroom than with happy hour at a beach hangout. Leisure is not about checking out and unwinding. It has nothing to do with vacation—a term derived from the Latin *vaco* meaning "to be empty or void." Vacation days are empty with nothing to do. Leisure is not emptiness or the absence of work or the removal of responsibility. It is not free time with nothing to do.

Leisure is about being gifted with the time necessary to be freed from doing hard work and being able instead to turn one's full attention to thinking about things that matter and then celebrating those things. And the things that matter and occupy the thoughts and efforts of those pursuing leisure are not how to make more money, purchase a bigger home, craft a more perfect vacation, or make winning wagers on one's preferred sports team. No, the thoughts afforded by leisure are focused on the contemplation of things that count: the purpose of life, the meaning of our humanity, the fulfillment of personhood, the significance of our relationships and our individual being, and our place in the creation immediately around us and within the entire universe. In other words, for Pieper leisure is the sort of deep thinking, wondering, and delighting done by philosophers, that is, "lovers of wisdom," who have been released from the constraints of merely sustaining life through hard labor and have arrived at a more profound grasp of what it means to exist as a sentient, self-aware, reflective being in the world.

Leisure entails much more than relaxing, and it is antithetical to doing nothing. Leisure means being fully aware and appreciative of the truths of the universe. It centers on knowing what it is to be alive and enjoying the continuing pursuit of greater understanding and appreciation of the reality animating the creation all around us—both the realities that we see and those not empirically verifiable. Leisure means living life in the fullness of our humanity and not merely surviving or indulging animal instincts. As noted, there is, then, a very real sense in which leisure contrasts with work. Hard work done to sustain life demands much in terms of effort and time and begrudges only meager leftovers of energy and interest for contemplation. Those who labor to survive don't have the luxury of lingering long in contemplation of things like the tingling anticipation and joy embedded in a summer sunrise. Those busy working are preoccupied with their tasks and are not free to revel in the defining significance and sheer marvel of the love, concern, and delight that bind them with the people who share their lives. Understood this way, a life that is preoccupied with the demands of work and that consequentially has no time for the pursuit of true leisure suffers a poverty deeper than financial lack. This is why the ancients considered manual labor to be subhuman activity. It was activity indistinguishable from that of animals. In the world of Plato and Aristotle, it was only a very small handful of people who enjoyed the necessary financial means that allowed the freedom of time to sustain noble human leisure. It is not so surprising then that leisure became associated with luxury and privilege, and, in the minds of many people, seemed to have more to do with trivial idleness than deep contemplation.

Pieper, though, understands and treasures the great depth and gift of genuine leisure as it was originally understood. And surveying his own twentieth-century context—when human ingenuity and discovery had finally made possible a world that for the ancients could be only a dream, a world in which one did not need to spend the bulk of every day working merely to survive—Pieper was appalled that people would continue to live lives shackled to their work. Watching the world frenetically at work rebuilding Europe after the ravages of a second world war in half a century, the German philosopher decried what he deemed a world of total work. At the moment when a life of genuine leisure was a real possibility for more than just a handful of elite aristocrats, people were choosing more and more work. Work and the tangible results of work had become not a means toward the greater end of true leisure but had become the ends themselves. And what was left of leisure was but a shabby façade of the great truth. Pieper wrote to rebuke and correct this tragedy that was unfolding around him, but writing in mid-century his focus was primarily on the problem of total work.

Seventy-five years later, in the early decades of the twenty-first century, there are likely many inclined to think Pieper's lament all but irrelevant. While the long-term effects are a story yet to be written, as noted in the previous chapter, one impact of the world's frantic reaction to the threat of a new virus and the resultant pandemic is the phenomenon of workers forsaking or dramatically curtailing their commitment to their jobs. It could be that the era of total work lamented by Pieper is now a thing of the past. But again, this remains to be seen. My own suspicion is that, in time, the importance of work will reassert itself once more. It is hard, after all, to battle and resist impulses hardwired into our being. So, while they may be more selective now in the work they choose, most of those who are eligible, I believe, will most likely find their way back to work, drawn to accomplish more in their lives than cultivating jigsaw-puzzle skills, dabbling in Mandarin, or binge-watching yet another "extraordinary" series about this or that. Nevertheless, and more to the point of this chapter, even if the aversion to a work-dominated life does maintain its traction, increase momentum, and become the new definition of ordinary existence in America, this replacement for a world of total work will be a far cry from a culture founded on leisure as championed by Pieper. That is to say, I am confident that Pieper would find very little to applaud in the Western culture that has evolved in twenty-first-century America. People in our world do not forsake work for the sake of contemplation and the pursuit of true human being; they spurn a life of total work so that they can devote themselves to the task of entertaining and amusing themselves. This is not leisure. This is the triumph of Rieff's psychological man.

THE PINNACLE OF LEISURE

There is a marked difference between our contemporary world's pursuit of diversion, entertainment, and merely sweetening the time and the idea of leisure as the contemplation and appreciation of what it means to be a human being living rightly in the creation. For Pieper, the goal or, as he puts it in his title, the "basis of culture" is certainly not diversion or entertainment; it is leisure that contemplates and celebrates the fullness of humanity. But Pieper pushes further in his defense of leisure, embellishing and enriching the classic understanding of leisure by emphasizing the essential spiritual aspects of leisure when it is rightly understood and practiced. Pieper contends that leisure cannot be realized without taking into account its necessary spiritual component. Indeed, for a person to live rightly related to the creation surrounding her, she must also live rightly related to the Creator above her who made her and every other creature. So it is that the highest and purest expression of leisure happens in the worship of God. Pieper expresses his rather remarkable conclusion this way: "But if celebration is the core of leisure, then leisure can only be made possible and justifiable on the same basis as the celebration of a festival. *That basis is divine worship.*"[2] Seen in this full light, the attraction of leisure as the key to the meaning of human existence becomes even more weighty for a Christian committed to living in tune with God's reality and will. The assertion that worship best exemplifies the ancient human aspiration for leisure is as surprising as it is compelling. Seen in this light, leisure is not exemplified by a handful of eggheaded philosophers exchanging profundities about the

2 Pieper, 65. Emphasis in original.

meaning of life or the secrets of the universe over Scotch and cigars; no, the essence of leisure is captured by the Christian worship of God.

For most Christians, this likely seems quite natural and on target. Indeed, the idea that the core of human being, the foundation for individual self-understanding, and the source of meaning for all of life is found in worship as the contemplation of God's truth and fellowship with God not only resonates with instinctive Christian piety but is confirmed repeatedly throughout the Bible. A few noteworthy instances should suffice as proof. On the mountain of Sinai, the elders of Israel delighted in the essence of leisure when they dined in the presence of God.[3] The Psalms overflow with the praise of God, and David explicitly and regularly cites the contemplation of God and his creation as part of his worship. David's prayer in Psalm 27 is particularly exemplary: "One thing I have asked from the Lord, that I shall seek: That I may dwell in the house of the Lord all the days of my life, to behold the beauty of the Lord and to meditate in His temple."[4] The prophet Isaiah expresses similar sentiments: "Your name, even Your memory, is the desire of our souls. At night my soul longs for You, indeed, my spirit within me seeks You diligently."[5] And the apostle Paul urges the Colossians, "Therefore if you have been raised up with Christ, keep seeking the things above, where Christ is, seated at the right hand of God. Set your mind on the things above, not on the things that are on earth."[6] The biblical evidence abounds.

Yet, perhaps the most widely and intuitively affirmed declaration of the Christian affinity for the classic idea of leisure is captured in the very first question and answer of the

3 See Exodus 24:1–2, 9–11.
4 Psalm 27:4. See also Psalms 8; 9; 84; 139; 143; 145.
5 Isaiah 26:8–9.
6 Colossians 3:1–2.

Westminster Shorter Catechism:

> Q: What is the chief end of man?
>
> A: Man's chief end is to glorify God and enjoy him forever.

To believers this all just sounds right. We are created to love and praise God and to live in harmony with him. From the very beginning when God strolled in the Garden of Eden and sought Adam and Eve to the culmination of the biblical story with all the saints gathered around the throne of God in John's Revelation, it seems clear that man is created to know and praise God.[7] A rich, classical understanding of leisure and faithful Christian confession seem to be entirely and wonderfully compatible with one another.

It is part of our essential human being to live in tune with God. We know it intuitively, and we find it confirmed in Scripture. This follows a common and repeated pattern in which there is a strong continuity between general revelation or the truths hardwired into the world around us and special revelation delivered by God through apostles and prophets. Truths that Aristotle learned through careful observation, discussion, and contemplation are reinforced and then more fully expressed and unfolded in the further revelation of God's direct words and actions as recorded in Scripture and articulated in Christian confession. The truths are simple but profound in their implications. Human beings are designed by God to do more than work; we are made for more than mere production. We are made to live in tune with God, with one another, and with all of creation. We are made for contemplation of the wonders of God's being and work. We are made to celebrate God and his glory. Once the

7 Genesis 3; Revelation 7.

concept has been fully articulated and seen in light of biblical truth, the claim seems obviously and eminently true: man's goal, his purpose, is aimed upward and outward to perfect fellowship and communion with God and his creation. In other words, as Pieper would put it, leisure is the basis of culture.

CELEBRATING THE FESTIVAL

With leisure's status now rehabilitated and even elevated to a place of priority, it is almost time to take the next step and consider the significance of the central and defining place of leisure. Before turning to that task, however, one more component of leisure needs a bit more attention. To round out the discussion and foster a full understanding and appreciation of leisure, and perhaps even to substantiate my claim that Pieper's explication of the classical and biblical understanding of leisure earns the status of "mind-blowing," we need to recognize the extraordinary breadth of leisure and its firm grounding in the material world. What makes the argument for the central significance of leisure particularly compelling, I think, is the idea mentioned in the quotation above, in which Pieper binds leisure with the idea of festival. *Festival* is a word that bears many meanings, churchly and otherwise. The "Festival of Easter" sounds safely and piously Christian and seems an appropriate expression of the decidedly spiritual aspect of leisure encouraged by Pieper, while the "Dogwood-Azalea Festival" of a small, southern Missouri city in the Mississippi River valley seems to resonate more with the relaxation and amusement ideas typically associated with leisure that this chapter has sought to overcome. But this twofold aspect of festival is precisely the point that needs to be made. The true beauty and power of the idea of leisure comes into focus when we refuse to make a sharp distinction between a secular and a sacred festival. To distinguish them is to make exactly the wrong move and will yield a wrong and misleading picture of leisure.

There is a real danger that one can begin to think of this classic, contemplative understanding of leisure, if not along the lines of a tediously highbrow conversation among intellectuals in a graduate seminar, then as a dreadfully wearisome and lifeless church service that seems never to end. This would be altogether mistaken. When rightly understood and practiced, leisure resembles neither. Leisure is not hedonistic amusement, but neither is it the stuff of arid irrelevant philosophers or insipid interminable worship. Leisure is not about something that happens only in your head or even in your heart. It is about a whole person living and delighting in a right relationship with her Creator and with all of the other creatures around her. It is a lived-out, exceedingly tangible reality expressed beautifully by the idea of festival founded on and flowing from worship and then celebrated with music, food, drink, games, laughter, handshakes, embraces, fireworks, and conversation. It looks a lot like people in a small community coming together for a few days of life out of the ordinary with no other objective than to celebrate their lives together.

Leisure is anything but boring and does not disdain the material realities of the world. It delights in them. And while it is sadly true that even the Midwest's smallest, most authentic, and honest towns have too often allowed their festivals to devolve into carefully crafted events orchestrated by the Chamber of Commerce in hopes of increasing the flow of cash into the hamlet, this was not always or originally the case. There was a time not so long ago when a town festival was nothing but a time of celebration for the sheer delight of being a community of people aiming at the same things in the same place at the same time. It might be the end of harvest, the appointed feast day of the local patron saint, or the commemoration of a singularly important event in the history of the place, but whatever the occasion, the festival meant a break from ordinary life. It was time outside of the routine and mundane reality with no other purpose than keeping and enjoying the festival itself.

Since the very essence of festival was a celebration of living together as God's creatures in God's extraordinary creation, the worship of God was the essential foundation of the festival. The 1621 harvest celebration of the Plymouth colonists and their Wampanoag neighbors provides an apt example. Prayers and praise of God were part of the festivities, but so was feasting on the bounty produced by fields and forest, along with games and singing and dancing. The core ingredients are consistent across cultures and times: worship, feasting, music, and games. It is not merely nostalgia or pining for days gone by that recognizes the goodness and beauty of such festivals; the wonder and importance of these festivals is apparent when seen through a right understanding of leisure. Festivals that begin in a mutual recognition and solemnization of God's gifts and lordship and then blossom into revelry and merrymaking that fuel warm memories and colorful stories for years to come are the very essence of leisure.

Not to be missed is the materiality, earthiness, and corporeality of festivals. Festivals are not sanitized spiritual affairs of the intellect or the emotions and are not geared toward mystical aspirations or yearnings. Festivals are bodily and physical. Good food is prepared and shared, favorite beverages abound, music fills the air and ears, games are won and lost, conversation loud and soft is abundant and punctuated with much genuine and joyful laughter. All these aspects of our material existence as creatures are recognized as good gifts of God and essential aspects of our human being. There is no room for a Gnostic-shaped suspicion of the tangible world and no disparagement of physical enjoyments. God has made us physical beings, after all—our corporeality is an essential part of our humanness. And God is also quite fond of using tangible material things—often the most common material things like water, bread, and wine—to deliver his grace. The incarnation itself is a standing reminder that God does not reject the physical reality of his creation; he joins himself to it by taking a human body into the Godhead. The physical and material aspects of festival are further reminders of the goodness of the creation and the Creator's delight in that creation. Leisure as festival helps express the depth of leisure that begins when man, as Pieper says, "consents to his own true nature and abides in concord with the meaning of the universe."[8] This captures the essence of leisure and of our humanity. It is difficult to imagine a more wonderfully potent or succinctly beautiful expression of what it means to be human. Man's true nature is body and spirit, and his universe is defined by those fellow creatures closest to him in his family and community. Genuine leisure tunes a person to live in harmony with this reality.

It is also worth noting that a festival takes work. Indeed, both the significance and success of any given festival are usually closely correlated with the amount of work invested in the festival. Even a family reunion demands an investment of time and money if it is going to take flight and achieve its objectives of celebrating God's gifts in and through the bonds of birth and marriage. A community-wide festival makes even greater demands on those ensuring its success. This truth sheds a further light on the complexity of true leisure. Leisure is not relaxing and doing nothing, yet neither is it working for

8 Pieper, 48.

the sake of production or monetary return. Those who work for the sake of a festival know that they are spending energy and resources for the sake of what produces no monetary return or capital improvement. And that is just the point. Leisure means investing hours, effort, and assets into a celebration that exists for its own sake but that does not exist without an expenditure. If this is starting to look and sound like work, then things are as they should be. Leisure cannot be construed as a simplistic moratorium on work, but it is also not work. The evident intricacy and apparent contradiction will get sorted out in due time, actually in the next chapter. For now, it is enough to recognize that genuine leisure rightly practiced involves the commitment of the whole creature with all that he has and is.

Finally, before wrapping up this discussion of festival and taking up a consideration of some implications and applications of a right understanding of leisure, Pieper insightfully observes that people cannot *not* have festivals. Human beings are so inexorably oriented to the need for festival that even those who reject any belief in, much less obligation of praise and gratitude toward, a divine Creator will fabricate festivals in a vain effort to manufacture the benefits and delights that are the essence of true festivals. So, cities declare victory parades to laud the championship season of their local professional sports team, corporations host obligatory "Holiday Season" (formerly Christmas) parties, unions sponsor picnics, and an array of specialized organizations formed to foster pride or protect rights of this or that group will sponsor festivals and events meant to pump up the esprit de corps and enhance public status. But these attempts at festivals all ultimately fail. They are counterfeits and frauds. Pieper gives the reason: "There is no such thing as a festival 'without gods'—whether it be a carnival or a marriage."[9] Indeed, writing in the middle of the twentieth century, Pieper's insights into man's proclivity for fake festivals is stunning. It's worth hearing him at length:

> Certainly we must ask whether the great epoch of artificial festivals is not still to come. Perhaps we should be preparing ourselves for it. Might we not expect the forces of society or, in the extreme case, the holders of political power to lavish tremendous effort on specious arrangements for the sake of artificially engendering a sham festivity—an illusory, semi-opaque semblance of "holidays" that would be devoid of the true and ultimate affirmation of the world that is the essence of the festive. Such holidays, moreover, are in fact based on suppression of such affirmation; they derive their dangerous seductiveness precisely from that.[10]

Pieper's prophetic words have unfolded as predicted. The world is doing its level best to conjure meaning and concoct festivals that ignore or even disparage God. Yet rather than reacting with indignation or disgust, Christians would better respond to the plethora of phony festivals with sorrow and pity. Those who crave depth and meaning for their living will not find it in an artificial festival that rejects the truth God has built into his creation. They need someone, they need God's people, to tell

9 Pieper, 65–66.
10 Ibid., 66.

them God's truth. Christians have much to offer to those around. No doubt, we have the good news of the gospel to proclaim, but we can also show our neighbors, who live for little yet yearn for much, what it looks like to celebrate a true festival that delights in both the Creator and his creation. This is the heart of true leisure and the essence of a life rightly lived.

ACEDIA

But humans struggle mightily to live rightly. It has been that way since the fall. Sin is our common lot; indeed, it is so common that we've even created lists of particularly problematic sins. None of those are more infamous than the seven cardinal sins, or vices. Given enough time, and a little prompting, most people are probably able to come up with all seven of the deadly sins. On the other hand, they generally have no success at all naming even two or three of the seven virtues, and even when told what they are, still have little idea what they mean—but that's a topic for another time.[11] The one that may trip some people up when listing the deadly sins is likely to be sloth. Somehow the sin of sloth doesn't quite register. Part of the problem is the name itself; in popular usage, *sloth* is reserved for the ultra-slow-moving, algae-coated mammal of Central and South American rainforests. But, interestingly, the animal was named for the vice and not the other way around. *Sloth* derives from "slow," and what other mammal moves more slowly or expends less effort than a sloth? It is an apt name for a creature whose curved claws hook onto branches with literally zero effort. The sloth's entire body becomes a living hammock suspended by the hook-claws—all that is needed is a nicely shaded branch.

11 For those trying to complete the lists, the seven deadly sins are pride, anger, envy, lust, gluttony, greed, and sloth; and the seven cardinal virtues are prudence, justice, courage, temperance, faith, hope, and love.

Even when one dies, a sloth's carcass will often remain hanging by its claws from that same branch. We are familiar enough with sloths in the trees but not familiar with the human sort. In our world, we rarely use the word *sloth* to describe people; we just call them lazy. That we equate slothfulness with laziness is probably the biggest reason people struggle to see the problem with sloth.

While the official list may declare sloth as a deadly sin, when we see it as the equivalent of laziness, we remain unconvinced of the danger. Laziness doesn't strike us as deadly. It seems not to be in the same category with other sins like anger, envy, or gluttony that might actually hurt us or other people. And while none of the seven deadly sins is technically illegal, sloth, when understood as mere laziness, seems to be particularly innocuous. The risk is just not immediately apparent. A lazy person may well be annoying, but it takes considerable imagination to create a scenario that makes the character flaw deadly. And yet our forebears in the faith saw in sloth a danger to be ranked among the very worst vices. They were convinced of this because they understood that sloth, or more accurately the idea that they recognized behind the label, was the betrayal of leisure.

In what has to rank in the top tier of odd twists in the development of language, modern English speakers typically associate *leisure* and *lazy* quite closely. While the words may not quite qualify as full-blown synonyms (at least, my thesaurus doesn't link them), they are certainly close cousins. The lazy person and the one enjoying leisure (as most English speakers commonly use the term) look little different and often overlap. And many people will use the adverbs *leisurely* and *lazily* as fully interchangeable. But laziness and true leisure, at least as it has been explained in this chapter, are actually antithetical to one another. It will help sort out the confusion between laziness and leisure by first sorting out the confusion between laziness and sloth. We begin that project by recognizing that the character fault of laziness is not the same thing as the vice labeled sloth. While the two shortcomings share some common ground and outward similarities, sloth is a failing that is far more substantial and definitive in its purview. To be lazy is to shun effort and to lack the initiative or ambition necessary to accomplish things. Laziness can certainly be an irritant to others, especially when those others are dependent on the lazy person to accomplish some task for them. And, in a culture of total work, or even one that just esteems work and productivity, to call someone lazy is rather a sharp rebuke, indeed. And yet laziness probably doesn't quite seem to belong to the class of moral failure. This is not to say that laziness is harmless or a character trait that shouldn't concern diligent parents—quite the opposite. Still, for most of us, a lazy person probably doesn't quite qualify as morally corrupt or deserving of utter condemnation. But if laziness doesn't damn, sloth does.

Sloth is the label that appears on the list of deadly sins, but it is a substitute for an older and even more uncommon word. That word is *acedia* (yes, it is in your dictionary), and while it is an old and obscure word, when it comes to naming the vice that ranks in the top seven, it is a better and more accurate word than sloth. This word choice is better because its very obscurity frees it from misleading assumptions or inaccurate connotations. It is more accurate because we are able to take this unfamiliar word and fill it with the meaning it carries from its ancient origins. Like so many of our English words, *acedia* comes to us from Greek. In fact, *acedia* is simply a cognate from the original Greek word *akēdia*. In this case, the *a*, or the alpha-privative, negates the noun *kēdia*, which means "to care." *Acedia*, in both English and its original Greek usage, then, means a lack of caring and a pervasive, life-draining indifference. So it is that the phrase "I don't care" may be less innocent than it seems and may actually carry negative moral freight. Perhaps this also affirms the intuitions of mothers—at least, certainly, in the instance of my wife—about what is best. Even before encountering the word *akēdia* or coming to a full appreciation of all that was involved in the deadly sin of acedia, my wife taught our children from the time they began having their first conversations that "not caring" was not an option, and the pat phrase "I don't care" was deemed out-of-bounds in our home. Teaching against indifference and nonchalance is teaching against acedia.

Understanding the ideas at work in the foundation of the word *acedia* points us in the right direction to guide us into the heart of the expansive and deadly realm that is the grave sin of acedia, a sin that is as unfamiliar in our culture as the word that names it. Acedia is a vice because this lack of caring and suffocating apathy stunts all positive interaction with the world and makes any *joie de vivre* utterly impossible (sorry for the French, but the phrase captures well the alacrity and zest that are the very "joy of living"). Acedia is, in other words, the opposite of leisure. This is why understanding acedia enriches and expands our grasp of the idea of leisure.

Acedia is not merely idleness or a sophisticated-sounding term for a shiftless and indolent person with expertise in evading effort. Acedia goes deeper. Acedia is the vice of the person who refuses to see and treasure his place as a human being within God's creation, who then cannot understand his purpose or the meaning of his life. Acedia is not the sin of doing nothing; it is the sin of failing to recognize what needs to be done and why it needs to be done. Acedia negates the very essence of what it means to be human. Apathy is certainly a component of acedia, but acedia is more than merely indifference. It is the studied and deliberate refusal to receive and honor the truths that are given in the fabric of the world. Acedia is anti-God, anti-creation, anti-human, and anti-festival. It opposes the very idea of a Creator who providentially directs and loves his work. It therefore forfeits the world as the product of a divine hand with a comprehensive and meaningful plan. The place and purpose of man as God's image and steward in the world and as created for fellowship with God and other creatures is thereby forfeited. And without God or an understanding of his will for creation, festivals can only be contrived and trivial.

Acedia may manifest itself in listlessness, inaction, and languor. On the outside, this looks like run-of-the-mill laziness. But the same vice can also foment a frenetic busy-ness that seems incapable of stopping or slowing for even a moment. The person who has despaired of the possibility of finding meaning in life may not necessarily collapse into a dismal shadow of torpid despondency but may instead cast away all restraint and escape the grasp of ennui and futility with a frenzy of busy doing, simply for the sake of doing something, anything. Hence the workaholic, the obsessed sports fanatic, the inveterate housecleaner, the compulsive video-gamer, and the chemically dependent addict may all, in their own particular and peculiar ways, be victims of the vice of acedia, even if they have never heard the word or considered the ideas it conveys. Whether it leads to indolent indifference or manic activity, acedia is always the vice of those who miss the meaning of life and so are unable to live in tune with God and with his creation. Considered within this frame it should be easier to see why acedia, or sloth, is indeed a grave and damning sin worthy to be counted among the top seven. When you are overcome by the vice of acedia, you are not being the creature you were created to be. You are denying your very being as a human.

In many ways, the sin or vice of acedia is but another way, albeit a very old way, to describe the very modern (though some insist on the distinction and call it postmodern) phenomenon of nihilism. In the nihilistic context in which all Westerners live, the taken-for-granted truths of the world and her people have all been challenged, cast under an impenetrable cloud of doubt and suspicion, and unequivocally designated as unproven and unproveable, leaving only personal convictions and sincere commitments to substantiate whatever truths are claimed. But when the only truth one can assert or claim is a truth that has been self-selected, then, in fact, no foundation for any conviction or any meaning in life can exist. All one ever has is a sincerely held idea that may or may not be tolerated, much less accepted, by others. Such a world is void of meaning. Such a world cannot sustain joy or host a genuine festival. Such a world creates, shapes, and names the vice of acedia. And acedia creates, shapes, and names such a world. It is neither possible nor necessary to determine which comes first. Both are a denial of the Creator and the meaning he infused into his world.

Nihilism is the empty philosophy that holds to nothing. Acedia is nihilism's pitiless partner. It is nihilism's sin of hopelessness, apathy, and despair which are but the bitter fruits of a life drained of meaning and left as an empty and impotent husk. If there is no certain truth, then there is no meaning in life, no reason to live, and no reason to bother with anything besides a vain effort to sweeten the time, amplify what bit of life remains, and insist on the happiness of autonomy and self-fulfillment.

But it is all pretense. The vice of acedia can deliver nothing but a fruitless search for meaning that cannot ever be found and a gnawing awareness of the vapid futility of a life that has no grounding beyond the self. Acedia and nihilism feed and reinforce one another. Acedia is the sin of the modern world. The person cursed with the vice of acedia is out of sync with God, with creation, and with himself. Acedia is the antithesis of leisure. And, as should be apparent, it is the antithesis of sabbath.

THE FACE OF LEISURE

By recognizing the smothering and life-draining tragedy of acedia, we can better appreciate the depth and breadth of true leisure. Leisure, remember, is rooted in the idea of scholia—indeed, *scholia* may well serve as a better term for the vital concept. Like *acedia*, *scholia* is an unfamiliar word ready to be filled with the right meaning. But whether we call it leisure or try to promote the word *scholia*, the idea is the same and is essential either way. Leisure, or scholia, is about more than rest and more than relaxing. It is about contemplation or, more accurately, a wisdom-based and wisdom-aimed discussion. It is about living in a studied and deliberate awareness of one's being and one's place in relationship to God and to the world he created. So, leisure is certainly expressed and practiced in worship. But leisure, or scholia, is also about delighting in, championing, and celebrating the realities of God and his creation; thus scholia is the very essence of festival.

When the sum of these ideas is considered, it becomes patently clear that leisure is in full harmony with all that is included in the idea of sabbath. Both sabbath and leisure are operating on the same ground. Bringing leisure, or scholia, together with sabbath has been the objective of this entire chapter, and that threshold has been reached. But before we enter finally and fully into that common space, sanctify that union, and conclude this chapter, there is one more layer of the rich meaning and vital importance of leisure that deserves particular attention. This is all the more the case given the short shrift this topic usually receives among Christians today. Though too often unrecognized and almost always unappreciated, aesthetics and the object of its attention, beauty, together play a critical part in understanding leisure. This means that beauty and its complementary field of inquiry known as aesthetics should similarly play more prominent roles in Christian thinking and living than they typically do. Like festivals, beauty (which figures prominently in festivals) plays a surprising but essential role in the practice and appreciation of leisure. It could be said that beauty is the face or visage of leisure; it is how scholia makes itself known or, more accurately, the way that leisure is experienced and felt.

While aesthetics should figure directly in a life lived well, for too many Christians, the term itself is unfamiliar and thoroughly mysterious. Not infrequently, aesthetics is simply confused with ethics, with people who first encounter the term assuming *aesthetics* is just a careless mispronunciation of *ethics*. Yes, I've seen it happen. Others who may actually have some notion that aesthetics deals with questions of beauty will make the unsurprising mistake of deeming the field elitist or highbrow and so distantly irrelevant for real life, perhaps labeling it as "something that philosophers or maybe artists and snobbish art collectors do, I think." This is typically the extent of most people's grasp of aesthetics. But while aesthetics is too often dismissed out of hand or misunderstood, it rightly belongs as a vibrant aspect of Christian faith and life. As suspected, aesthetics is indeed rightly understood as a branch of philosophy. As the dictionary puts it, aesthetics is a "set of principles concerned with the nature and appreciation of beauty, especially in art; or the branch of philosophy that deals with the [same]."[12] So while philosophers and artists have an interest in aesthetics, and beauty that lies at the center of the work of aesthetics, why should ordinary Christians be particularly concerned about either?

The answer lies in some big ideas that lurk under and over all of existence. These are ideas that have been recognized, discussed, affirmed, and revered by people for thousands of years. In this case, I'm referring to the ideas or concepts of the three transcendentals: truth, goodness, and beauty. Although pagan philosophers like Plato and Aristotle lacked the benefit of direct divine revelation, they nevertheless thought hard about what the world itself revealed to them. By paying attention to the realities that the Creator had built into the world, ancient lovers of wisdom may not have known the source, but they did know that the fundamental ideas of truth, goodness, and beauty were at work in the world as norms and goals for all of existence and were not simply the product of mere human whim. Truth was the fundamental *real* that a person should know and embrace. Goodness was the foundational *right* that a person should desire and do. And beauty was the *ravishing* or *radiant* that a person should cherish and enjoy. The ancients concluded that human being was fulfilled by striving for and reaching a right relationship with the transcendentals.

Christianity dismisses the notion of the upward climb and rejects the idea that man can, by his own effort, find his way to the fullness of the transcendentals—the realities that undergird, direct, and fulfill all of creation. Christian teaching certainly

12 *New Oxford American Dictionary* (Apple Dictionary app, version 2.3.0), s.v. "aesthetics."

does not champion personal striving and self-perfection but celebrates grace given by God. But Christianity also acknowledges that the ancients weren't entirely wrong to detect the reality of the transcendentals of truth, goodness, and beauty at work in the world. Christians confess that truth, goodness, and beauty belong to God and were built into the world in his work of creating. And when, according to the eternal plan, God becomes incarnate, it is then that his grace is made concrete, and the transcendentals are embodied and fully revealed in the truth, goodness, and beauty of Jesus Christ. What is true, what is good, and what is beautiful are all found in their fullness in Christ. Those who receive his grace and live as his followers encounter and learn to celebrate the wonders of truth, goodness, and beauty.

The above synopsis is necessarily brief—after all, this is not exactly a book about the transcendentals or even beauty.[13] Still, an understanding and appreciation of all three transcendentals can greatly enhance our grasp of leisure, or scholia. To delight in leisure is to know the truth, practice goodness, and love the beautiful. All three of these foundational components of creation are tied to a right practice of leisure. I believe, though, that beauty and the intentional study of beauty that we call aesthetics particularly deserve special attention and emphasis in the church. This emphasis is needed simply because beauty and its importance for human living and even Christian faith is so routinely and thoroughly ignored by most Christians, especially those in my own corner of the church catholic. Even if

13 The three transcendentals are an essential though now often overlooked aspect of understanding the world and the way that it works. They deserve a great deal more attention also in the church. I'll take up the discussion of the transcendentals again a bit more fully in chapter 7, but a truly adequate exploration would amount to the work of another entire book.

they don't recognize the terminology, Christians don't entirely neglect the transcendentals. The Christians I know are keenly interested in questions of truth. They are determined to discern and hold tenaciously to right teaching. This is a good focus, of course. Doctrine does matter. What a person believes and confesses is naturally of paramount importance. For those believers who especially prize right doctrine, like conservative Lutherans, knowing and teaching the truth of God's revelation through orthodox creeds and confessions is the obvious core of Christianity, and so the transcendental of truth ranks high.

The transcendental of goodness is also granted significance in the church—even, at least to some extent, in my Lutheran orbit. But for many Christians, especially those I know, matters of goodness or what is right do not garner quite the same degree of zeal or attention as do questions about truth or what is real. The reason is obvious enough: goodness has to do with *doing* what is right, which has to do with good works, which tumbles into questions about morality—and for too many Lutheran believers, issues focused on moral behavior are often met with suspicion, since the pursuit of the good seems somehow to be at odds with grace and may even smack of works-righteousness. The resultant tepid enthusiasm for questions of goodness comes, then, as no surprise. But if the pursuit of truth is applauded, and the cultivation of goodness is tolerated, the delight in beauty is all but nonexistent. Somehow Christians have come to believe that doctrine is essential, ethics are acceptable, but aesthetics are optional—at best. This is wrong. It misses the inherent interconnections and threefold nature of the transcendentals and overlooks the church's own long and right history emphasizing all three transcendentals.

Much more could be said about the singular importance of aesthetics for Christian confession, but making that case worthily would far exceed the limits of this book and likely the patience of the reader.[14] For now, my hope is to raise the issue and nudge Christians to give a bit more thought to the place of beauty. It would be a significant step in the right direction if believers were even half as sensitive to questions of beauty as they are to issues of truth and goodness. What is true and good is beautiful, and what is beautiful is true and good. Beauty is not merely in the eye of the beholder; like truth and goodness, beauty accords with, declares, and revels in God's plan built into the fabric of his creation. Christians should seek out, praise, study, enjoy, and share what is beautiful. And this should be the case not only in their corporate places of worship but also in their homes and workplaces.

This is not meant to imply that massive outlays of money are required—quite the opposite. Often, what is most beautiful is what is altogether simple and common. But what is foolish, superficial, or trite works against beauty, even if it might not be entirely ugly. Kitsch dishonors the Creator and the beauty of his creation because it does not resonate with God's reality or his will for his creation. What is banal or contrived or tawdry, even when attempted as sacred art or religious expression, actually points away from the truth and goodness of God. What is beautiful, however, points us to the wonder of God and his grace and glory, and it encourages us to revel in the wisdom and creativity he has revealed to us in and through the creation. Beauty is a matter of the eye, no doubt, but it involves all the senses. Beautiful sounds, textures, tastes, and smells are all within the

14 There is not exactly a glut of good books on the subject of aesthetics, especially not from the perspective of Christian confession. A decent place to start might be Roger Scruton's *Beauty: A Very Short Introduction* (Oxford: Oxford University Press, 2011); Frank Burch Brown's *Religious Aesthetics: A Theological Study of Making and Meaning* (Princeton: Princeton University Press, 1989); or Jonathan King's *The Beauty of the Lord: Theology as Aesthetics* (Bellingham, WA: Lexham Press, 2018).

purview of a creature seeking to live in tune with the profound and sublime wonders that establish, pervade, and adorn God's remarkable creation. Beauty matters. The Christian life and witness must invest attention and concern not only in what is true and what is good but also in what is beautiful. Beauty is an essential part of the practice of leisure; and so aesthetics, which explores beauty and trains us better to love and appreciate beauty, also deserves a place in our lives.

At least one implication of this focus on aesthetics is a greater appreciation for art. Art, whether visual or auditory or linguistic, is not merely an enhancement to life. It is not a luxury to be added after the necessary is accomplished. Art is not an activity only for the elite or a handful of talented people. Rather, we need to understand art as an essential practice for being human. When art is functioning as it should—and in the modern world in which we all live, we are well aware that it is not often meeting this standard—art is the task of making God's reality, his truth and his goodness and his beauty, manifest in the world. In the utter and overwhelming pragmatism of the West—a cultural character trait seemingly brought to its apex in the United States—good art that points to the transcendentals established by God needs to be supported and celebrated with particular resolve and intention. Christians should set the standard for their support of faithful art. Art matters because it celebrates beauty. And the celebration of beauty is in a sense simply another way to describe the practice of leisure, or scholia. Truth is the mind of leisure, goodness is its strength, and beauty is the heart and spirit of leisure. Art is the practice of making these things known in the world; and so, beautiful art is the expression and aura of leisure. And finally, aesthetics plays its part by teaching us and forming us to live more fully in the joy of God's beauty and the art that expresses that beauty.

CONCLUSION

Leisure is the contemplation, recognition, and celebration of God and his reality. It revels in truth, goodness, and beauty. Seen in this light, it is clear that true leisure is not only completely unrelated to the leisure suit that haunts my high school memories but the truth is that the two are actually antithetical. Leisure delights in beauty; the leisure suit denigrates it. The leisure suit may not be the nadir of ugliness, but it lurks in the vicinity of those depths. To think of leisure as a great good, indeed as the purpose and target of human living, may still seem an unusual idea. And if the word itself presents too great a barrier to such thinking, then scholia is ready for your use—though that might not be much of an improvement. Whatever signifier is used, the core idea is vital. Josef Pieper is right to call it the basis of culture. But leisure is not, then, a panacea ready at hand to solve the emptiness or ennui of the culture around us. Leisure is not a life-hack for a nihilistic world. It is not the secret to unlock a meaningful life. It is not the philosophical or theological equivalent of "mindfulness" that can be worked into a life shaped by other forces, goals, and priorities to give it just the right balance or extra boost of spiritually that it was lacking. Pieper makes this point explicitly as he concludes his reflections on leisure: "Leisure cannot be achieved at all when it is sought as a means to an end, even though that end be 'the salvation of Western civilization'."[15] Leisure is not a tool to be used; it is the reality that lies at the heart of human existence. One either lives in tune with the reality of leisure and receives its truth, goodness, and beauty, or he forfeits the gift in his pragmatic effort to "make things work." To instrumentalize leisure is to lose it.

Leisure begins with the Creator and then expands outward to engage all of creation. It centers on the key interface between

15 Pieper, 72.

the individual, his Lord and Master, and the world around him. So the practice of leisure is the practice of being human as God intended. It correlates directly with the two kinds of righteousness—before God and before the world—just at it correlates with the transcendentals of truth, goodness, and beauty upon and within which the Creator grounded his masterwork of creation. Seen in the light of these truths, leisure's connection with sabbath should be evident. Sabbath was the endpoint of the Creator's work just as leisure is the culmination of human being. The practice of keeping sabbath is the celebration of what God has accomplished and our delight in being a part of God's work; similarly, leisure revels in the wonderful delight that we are invited to participate in the truth, goodness, and beauty that God has infused into the reality of his creation. Sabbath points us forward to the final consummation when all of creation will again be living in harmony, just as leisure reminds us that the unity and oneness we taste now is but an anticipation of the fullness that will come at the eschaton, when Christ returns in glory and makes all things new. Receiving and embracing sabbath and leisure is indeed the basis of culture and of human living. It serves not only as goal and purpose but as grounding and comfort in the midst of our broken world and harried lives. The lives of God's people will be enriched and empowered when leisure regains its fitting place. It is a great gift waiting to be discovered, enjoyed, extended, and shared.

Given the vast scope and significance of leisure and seeing how exquisitely and exhaustively it answers the big questions of human existence, it might well seem that nothing else is left to be done and the objective of this book has been achieved. Josef Pieper might say as much. But we are not blessed with so neat and tidy a resolution to the question of human existence and the meaning of life. We cannot declare leisure as the end and be done. Indeed, given the argument of the previous chapter on work, the argument of this chapter on leisure presents a rather significant quandary: How can work be an ontological aspect of human being and at the same time leisure be the fulfillment and highest expression of human being? Pieper saw work as the enemy of leisure, and those who espouse vocation often identify the inaction of leisure as the great vice that threatens a rightly shaped life. So, in two successive chapters, full-throated affirmation has been given to two apparently mutually exclusive and conflicting ideas. Is it possible that work is essential to our human being and that leisure is the point of our lives? How can these polarizing ideas be reconciled? Clearly, there is work that remains to be done.

reason for
live the
Down & Out Life.

Delighting in the Down and Out Life

Day 7: Embracing God's Sabbath Gift
work, rest, or play
Re-thinking Sabbath

Joy fully living
Down and Out
Life and the Joy
Brings

Design for the Down and Out

Sabbath and the Meaning of Existence

The Point of it All

Your Reason for Being

Sabbath Work: Re-Thinking God's Rest

God's Plan for

Receiving God's

CHAPTER 5

THE RECEPTIVE LIFE

MEANING IN LIFE

George Orwell published his famous novel *1984* in 1949. Seventeen years earlier, Aldous Huxley offered his own alarming version of the future of humanity in his equally famous, or perhaps infamous, *Brave New World*. Both novels routinely top any list of literature designated as dystopian.[1] Dark and foreboding references to Orwell's "Big Brother" are a mainstay when one feels the need to deploy heavy-handed verbiage designed to malign or vilify some deserving target—usually on the right end of the political spectrum—that is deemed guilty of oppression. It seems, though, that one hardly ever encounters similar alarms or aspersions linked to Huxley's "soma," the happiness-inducing and compliance-ensuring drug that was ubiquitous and essential for every aspect of the society of his novel. Now that the twenty-first century has arrived, our Western contemporaries appear to be far more concerned about the potential horrors of an Orwellian Big Brother future than they are about living in a *Brave New World* future as described by Huxley. Perhaps that is because in many ways, Huxley's prognosis seems to have been far more accurate—at least in our world of the Enlightenment West. While we may not yet have reached the full flower of Huxley's genetically manipulated subspecies within *Homo sapiens* and all babies asexually decanted from bottles, we are quite well along our way to a society obsessed with unencumbered sexual gratification

1 Given the amount of attention I've given to the meaning of words, it is impossible to ignore a fascinating word like *dystopia*. Coined by Thomas More in 1516, *Utopia* was the title of his book on an imaginary ideal world. *Utopia* literally means "not a place" or "no place." Perhaps it was More's not-so-subtle implication that an idyllic perfect place is by definition a fiction. On the other hand, a dystopia is presumably a "bad place," and while maybe not quite an antonym of utopia, it is certainly a disappointing and nasty version of the ultimate perfect place.

and artificially generated instant happiness that obscures and deflects all present pain. People may debate whose dystopia is more historically grounded, more terrifying, or more technologically feasible, but from my perspective there is no question which author most accurately anticipated the trajectory of Western culture: Huxley's version is far more recognizable in our world today than is Orwell's.

Five years after he published *Brave New World*, Huxley released a decidedly nonfiction philosophical text, *Ends and Means*, which, as the subtitle put it, was *an enquiry into the nature of ideals and into the methods employed for their realization*. It is a fascinating book. Huxley's fresh and sometimes surprising exploration of classic themes and questions about human existence cements his status as a significant and insightful thinker. But what makes him particularly compelling, at least to me, is his candor. Huxley is disarmingly, even startlingly, honest about the thoughts and motivations that drove his own philosophical positions on moral truth and its foundation—or as he hoped, lack of the same. The sort of strange, or brave new, world Huxley created in his novel with its wildly unconventional moral code frequently confuses even those who try to explain the book. In Huxley's novel, the sexually libertine and promiscuous protagonists are not deviants or immoral but are actually conforming to the moral code of the day—a code founded not on ideals such as self-control, sacrifice, marriage, and family but on the new ideals of self-indulgence, pleasure, individuality, and the elimination of pain. In *Ends and Means*, Huxley divulges rather bluntly that this new list of ideals was also at work already in the twentieth century. He needs to be heard at length:

> I had motives for not wanting the world to have a meaning; and consequently assumed that it had

> none, and was able without any difficulty to find satisfying reasons for this assumption. . . . The philosopher who finds no meaning in the world is not concerned exclusively with a problem in pure metaphysics. He is also concerned to prove that there is no valid reason why he personally should not do as he wants to do. . . . For myself, as no doubt, for most of my contemporaries, the philosophy of meaninglessness was essentially an instrument of liberation. The liberation we desired was simultaneously liberation from a certain political and economic system and liberation from a certain system of morality. We objected to the morality because it interfered with our sexual freedom; we objected to the political and economic system because it was unjust. The supporters of these systems claimed that in some way they embodied the meaning (a Christian meaning, they insisted) of the world. There was one admirably simple method of confuting these people and justifying ourselves in our political and erotic revolt: we could deny that the world had any meaning whatsoever.[2]

What is so interesting about this quotation is that it humbles

2 Aldous Huxley, *Ends and Means: An Enquiry into the Nature of Ideals and into the Methods Employed for Their Realization* (New York: Harper, 1937), 312, 315, 316.

the heady work of philosophy by unceremoniously dragging it down to earth and the basics of human existence that actually matter: the need to find and legitimize a workable way of being human each day. Huxley found that answer by capitulating to his desires manifest in sexual license, and then vindicated and normalized his answer by asserting the elimination of any ground for morality beyond the person. A world without meaning meant a world with no morality beyond the cultivation and amplification of pleasure—but respectably practiced, to be sure, within an enlightened and permissive social context where the behavior could be marketed as socially and even morally commendable and so could gain the support of others with equally sophisticated and compliant minds. This is, of course, precisely the premise for *Brave New World*, which, if they are honest, probably doesn't strike most people as entirely dystopian.

So, why is Huxley, and his version of the future with an alternate morality, relevant in a book about work, leisure, and sabbath? Huxley is important, I think, because his five-hundred-years-into-the-future prognosis, written between the world wars in the last century, has come to fruition in remarkable ways already in this century. Huxley's culture—in which sexual license is not an aberration but an expectation, in which marriage and children are routinely treated as unnecessary embellishments for a life that is oriented instead to personal fulfillment, in which that fulfillment is premised on the maximizing of any and every pleasure bounded only by the rights of others to do the same, and in which a necessarily elaborate legal system exists to adjudicate and manage the boundary between individual rights—has, in fact, become the very definition of our world today. And the foundation on which this new alternate morality is being built is precisely the one championed by

Huxley: a confident declaration that the world holds no meaning. We are now living in the kind of world that results when all meaning has been evacuated from human existence. And while there are, no doubt, still those who find life without a foundation and without moral parameters breathtakingly exhilarating, there are increasing numbers of people who recognize life in this kind of world to be insipid, pointless, and dehumanizing.

All of this is tied, certainly, to the modern dismissal of God as the source and authority of all life. Once God has been removed from the picture, the standard for morality also collapses, and the remaining vacuum is then swiftly and artificially filled with shifting moralities premised on individual freedom, presumed rights, and personal pleasure. But this all amounts to the most extreme form of autopoiesis—that is, a self-created reality and a self-chosen morality. This self-generated morality is inherently disastrous and essentially self-defeating since it lacks the one thing essential for a moral system: a standard and authority beyond the self. But knocking meaning out of the world not only opens the door for the creation of a flexible morality as Huxley intended, but it also inflicts on every person living in such a world the collateral damage of there being no purpose for human living beyond whatever meaning each person is individually able to muster or manufacture. Meaning and purpose in life is reduced to mere personal choice—or more accurately, finding meaning in life becomes the obligatory project of each person. And, as those who try it inevitably learn, if what matters is nothing more than what I choose, then it doesn't actually matter, even to the one who chose it. The lack of meaning in the world, and so also in a human life, that Huxley embraced as his ticket to a new, sexually permissive morality has become precisely the greatest crisis of the world in which we now live. That great crisis is my concern; it is conscientiously in the crosshairs of this book. My effort to unpack and more fully articulate work, leisure, and sabbath is meant as an answer to the problem of human purpose. God's truth fully solves the crisis of meaning and eradicates the crisis. Bringing meaning to human living is one of the great gifts delivered when we learn well God's plan for our lives in terms of work, leisure, and sabbath.

THE CHRISTIAN ANSWER(S)

Christians know exactly where to look to find more than enough meaning and purpose to last a lifetime. Meaning does not come from within; it must be delivered from outside. It is established by the one who created the world. Those who confess Christ have been taught what is also self-evident to anyone not heedlessly, relentlessly committed to willful blindness by cynical agendas—like Huxley. Christians know that there is a Creator, who built the world with forethought according to a precise plan. But, unlike those who merely believe in some divine power or force that must drive the beginning and lie as the foundation of the universe, Christians also know that the God who created is a personal God, who is thoroughly invested in his creation, continuously and solicitously guiding and sustaining it.

This means that discerning human purpose and meaning in life is not a project to be accomplished or a mystery to be unraveled; it is simply a truth to be received. God gives and his creatures receive. The Creator speaks and creatures listen—until they don't. It began with Adam and Eve, and it has not stopped. Every human has inherited the propensity of our first parents. We don't listen to God. In fact, in the shattered reality of our sinful condition, we humans have so stopped up our ears against

God's speaking that we can hear nothing of the divine voice without God's gracious intervention. The Holy Spirit must force open ears slammed shut in stubborn disbelief. Those who continue to resist and reject the Spirit's earnest work are doomed to remain deaf to God's Word and compelled to find or conjure their own interpretations and understandings of their human lives and the world around them. Huxley serves as a poster child of this sorry enterprise, but their number is legion. Indeed, every person in all of creation who lives apart from God's revelation in Christ is sentenced to the same weary task of securing some semblance of meaning to somehow salvage an otherwise futile existence.

It is hardly surprising that people who arrogantly refuse to accept and believe what God has revealed are compelled to live without meaning and purpose unless they manufacture it themselves. What is more difficult to understand is that even those who know God's grace, seek to live in the Spirit, and listen for God's voice too often also struggle to hear rightly what God has to say. Those who claim to follow Christ are also susceptible to making a mess of the message that God speaks. They are also prone to lose the meaning and purpose for life that God offers and instead become preoccupied with crafting their own answers to the meaning of life. The quest to settle the problem about the meaning and purpose of life is a helpful way of understanding the fraught situation that defined Luther's world as he struggled to find peace with God. In one sense, citizens of the sixteenth century did not have to wonder about life's purpose. They were reminded of it continually: live well to escape hell. And living well meant following the dictates of the church. Still, already well before the Reformation, there was a lack of consensus on the best way for a person to spend life in preparation for eternity. What exactly it meant to live rightly was not a settled question—not even within the church.

In Luther's day, the church offered two basic tracks for understanding human existence and purpose. Either one lived according to the prescription of the *vita activa* or one embraced the guidance offered by the *vita contemplativa*. At their most basic, the two distinct routes boiled down to exactly what their Latin terms indicate. A person either worked hard doing tangible things, accomplishing acts of service in the world, and so accumulating an archive of good works or a person secured right standing with God and a secure eternal future by devoting himself as entirely as possible to spiritual reflection, pious and sincere worship, and upward-reaching union with God. Either a person worked his way into heaven or he worshiped his way into heaven. Living in Luther's day, you would choose either the life of activity or the life of contemplation.

The debate between the two ways of approaching life ebbed and flowed and was never fully settled. Though, for most common people, there was little question; faced with things that needed to be done simply to survive, people lived lives of activity and left contemplation for those who had forsaken life in the world for a life centered on worship, reflection, and spiritual ascent in the cloister. Yet even those in the monasteries were not in agreement on the best way forward. Some consciously forsook all earthly work and gave themselves fully and only to prayer and spiritual pursuits, others gave themselves wholeheartedly to serving the world around, and still others strove to balance the two ways.

Given the extended discussions in two previous chapters of this book—one dedicated exclusively to work followed by another dedicated entirely to a consideration of leisure or contemplation—it seems that the progression of this book has arrived at much the same place, and we find ourselves confronted with the dilemma of the old ecclesiastical debate. Is the best formula for a meaningful and purposeful life a zealous focus on working, or is the best path to fullness and significance a focus on contemplating? Is the basic purpose of life active work in tune with the world, or is the basic purpose leisurely contemplation in fellowship with God? Should Christians pursue the *vita activa*, or should they be embracing the *vita contemplativa*?

Actually, this way of phrasing the problem fails miserably. The right path forward is not to decide in favor of one or the other of these two ways. But the way forward is also not the discovery of some creative and compelling way to reconcile or balance these two alternatives. Whether choosing between them or creatively blending them, a critical mistake is inevitably made. Both of these approaches to life, the *activa* and the *contemplativa*, commit the same fatal error: they focus primary attention on the self. Balancing or blending them does nothing to correct this fundamental problem of wrong focus; the egocentricity inherent in both approaches to life remains intact. The problem with both of these old, well-traveled pathways to a meaningful life is that both are preoccupied with what the self does or does not do. They are alike in putting the individual person at the center. Whether the person is busily working or prayerfully contemplating, what that person is doing or not doing is the essential thing. The person remains the focus of his own efforts, forever questioning: "Am I working hard enough at the right things?" or "Am I sincere and fervent enough in my prayers seeking God?"

The preoccupation with self is a deep and persistent temptation of, and far too often also a failing of, Christian people. And it is certainly not just Christians who endured the harsh rigor of medieval life long ago who lived lives that were far too concerned with their own performance. Some of today's most zealously pious and ardent disciples of Jesus fall into the same self-absorbed trap. They become so intent on the things they must do or not do, so interested in their progress or their accomplishments, or so overwrought with their shortcomings and failures that they have little room left for anything else. Like the Christians of Luther's day, these believers' lives are centered around the project of themselves. They strive to meet this or that standard, press forward to achieve some benchmark or another, or obsess over following whatever prescription or proscription they have most recently adopted as the thing that most matters. Those with a bent toward biblicism or who are eager to attest to what they are convinced is confessional faithfulness or who want to prove their zeal for teaching that they deem to be traditional are particularly susceptible to this peculiar temptation to self-absorption. The problem is that the very effort at self-improvement and the attempt to follow the right path compels a person to focus inward in order to assess progress. The solution for the problem of finding meaning and purpose for life does not lie in the direction of the *vita activa*, the *vita contemplativa*, or a mixture of the two. A different path that leads away from an occupation with self is needed.

THE VITA RECEPTIVA

Luther provides that path. Some have argued that Luther's contribution was to navigate a synthesis between the two ways and endorse this blended option as a *vita passiva*. The idea of passivity is certainly a step in the right direction as it moves the emphasis away from the self that dominates both the *vita activa* and the *vita contemplativa*. Luther consistently and emphatically asserted the passivity of man when it comes to questions of salvation—man contributes nothing in his standing before the Creator. In that relationship, man is indeed wholly passive, and God takes the spotlight, as is appropriate. But the reformer offered very different counsel when the context shifted from heaven to the creation all around and considered a person's relationships and duties in everyday life. In his life in relation to the world, Luther was quite clear; a man needs to engage with active zeal in the tasks he has been given to do. Passivity is ruled out. So, the idea of a *vita passiva* as a concept that can encompass the whole of the Christian life is inadequate because it fails to account for the very active part of Christian living that actually comprises the bulk of ordinary life spent interacting with other creatures. To better capture Luther's actual teaching about the dynamic of the Christian life, I would suggest the term *vita receptiva*, the receptive life.

Vita receptiva is a particularly apt label for Luther's understanding of the Christian life because it accounts for both the vertical and the horizontal components of Christian living. Luther completely reversed everything people assumed to be true about the purpose of life, sweeping away any remnant of pious obsessing over progress in the upward climb toward God in the vertical realm, whether through purposeful action or through prayerful contemplation. Instead, Luther insisted, the Christian simply receives what God gives. The Christian is saved, as Article IV of the Augsburg Confession so succinctly and accurately puts it, by grace through faith in Jesus Christ alone. Salvation is simply reception of what God gives. And then, when the fully redeemed believer turns once more to the tasks of life waiting to be done in this world, he is yet again fully receptive. The believer receives as gifts from God the particular relationships in which he lives his life, shoulders the attendant responsibilities of each vocation, and strives to live his life in obedience to the will of God, which he receives with gratitude from his Lord and Creator. He is receptive to the work God assigns and receptive to the way that God desires it to be done. The idea of the *vita receptiva* conveys the reality that holds true in each realm and achieves what is, from the standpoint of Luther's teaching, the most important objective of eliminating the individual self as an object of concern.

Without using the term *vita receptiva*, Luther expresses the ideas just described with delightful clarity in his 1520 essay *Freedom of the Christian*. Here Luther argues for the twofold nature of the Christian life but emphasizes that this life is not focused on self; rather it is focused outside oneself:

> We conclude, therefore, that a Christian lives not in himself, but in Christ and in his neighbor. Otherwise he is not a Christian. He lives in Christ through faith, in his neighbor through love. By faith he is caught up beyond himself into God. By love he descends beneath himself into his neighbor.[3]

This extraordinary quote from Luther has come to rank as one of my favorites from the reformer—and with Luther's gift for quotable prose, that is saying a great deal. What I find so compelling about this brief passage is the absolute disinterest of the Christian in his own performance, progress, or standing before God or before the world. Each Christian is called to live entirely outside of himself—living in Christ by

3 Martin Luther, *Luther's Works*, vol. 31, *Career of the Reformer*, ed. Harold J. Grimm (Philadelphia: Fortress Press, 1957), 371. Used by permission of Augsburg Publishing House.

faith and receiving from him grace that grants full salvation that then sends him out into the world to serve his neighbor. The Christian does nothing for himself; he only receives and then gives. The Christian is completely liberated from all anxious calculating, endless performing, or desperate negotiating done in an impossible effort to gain peace and assurance before God by his own effort. All that each Christian needs is fully and finally supplied in Christ. The believer is caught up into God by the gracious work of Christ to whom he clings in faith. And then, with all settled before God, the focus turns fully to the neighbor, and again the Christian's individual self is ignored. The only and all-consuming focus is now the neighbor. Love means the doing of good works. Love means following God's will for life. Love means dying to self and living for the sake of the other. Love means receiving the neighbor and her needs as gifts directly from God and then selflessly pouring out one's own self to meet the neighbor's needs. This is the heart of the Christian life: the reception of grace from God for salvation and then purposeful direction from God for vocation. This is the *vita receptiva*.

In the remote chance that you are not fond of the penchant of theologians for designating key ideas with Latin shorthand, in more colloquial English you could also say that understanding the Christian life as receptivity is seeing Christianity as a "down and out" life. God finds the broken and helpless sinner just where he is in the pit of death and despair and does not demand that he pull himself up and climb out or offer him a hand up to get him moving. No, Christ comes to us and does it all, carrying us into the peace, glory, and joy of his eternal kingdom. God's grace flows down from God through Christ to the repentant believer; and then love flows out from the believer to the neighbor. It is the down and out life. Saturated in Christ's flood of grace, the remade creature is sent out into the creation to serve the creation as God always intended. The freed Christian is uncurled from his perpetual pillbug-like posture. No longer curled and wrapped tightly in on himself and preoccupied with his own needs and progress, he is now faced out into the world and steps out purposefully and confidently to serve his neighbor in that world. God's grace is received, and God's task is received. And the individual self of the Christian believer does not enter into the calculation at all. The believer gives no heed to himself whatsoever. This is the beauty of the *vita receptiva*. This is the wonder of the down and out life. This is Luther's great gift to the church: not the invention of but the restoration of this faithful and powerful understanding of the Christian life as an essential part of orthodox Christian teaching.

RESOLVING THE CONFLICT

In chapter 3, I concluded that it is correct to understand work as an ontological aspect of what it means to be human. Grasping the significance of man's creation in God's image means recognizing that God equipped and directed his human creatures to fulfill their responsibility to care for his new creation. Specifically, they were to have dominion over the creation; Adam was placed into the garden to subdue it, that is, to tend it and cultivate it. This meant that from the very beginning, Adam was created to work. To work is an essential part of being human. Having declared human labor as an ontological reality, I went in a completely different direction in chapter 4 and offered an endorsement of the insights of Josef Pieper and his ardent argument for the reclamation of leisure and the repudiation of a world of total work. Leisure, or scholia, was asserted to be the very telos of human being, the reason for human existence.

Man was created to live in harmony with God and, through contemplation of God and his works, celebrate true leisure. Given the two diametrically opposed guiding theses of each chapter, a rather spectacular collision seems inevitable. The conviction that man is created to work and the equally adamant assertion that man is created for contemplation and worship seem irreconcilable. Pieper says as much in his rejection of a culture of total work; and we have seen that for their part, those who are committed to work and vocation as the point of life are deeply suspicious of shirkers who loiter through life or retreat into mere spirituality that shuns the mundane work waiting to be done. To state the obvious, work as ontology maps rather neatly to a *vita activa* outlook on life, while leisure as human fulfillment correlates with a *vita contemplativa* approach to life. As it was in the Middle Ages, the contention between them would appear to be interminable.

Nevertheless, as the reader has certainly anticipated, but continuing in the spirit of stating the obvious, my assertion is that the Lutheran understanding of the *vita receptiva* applies also here in the debate between work and leisure and allows us to see that these two very different outlooks on the meaning and purpose of human life are not hopelessly irreconcilable or irretrievably locked in bitter conflict. Though it will no doubt come as a disappointment to those who relish a good duel, there is no need to schedule the obligatory grudge match so that work and leisure can square off for a fight to the finish and a clear winner emerge from the dust. I argued above that the *vita receptiva* should not be construed as a compromise or blending of the active and contemplative approaches to life. Similarly, the way to navigate the opposing ideas of work as ontology and leisure as the human telos is not to knock off a few sharp angles from each so that they better cooperate nor to confine each to an insulated silo safely out of the way of the other approach. The better way is to let both of these compelling and prescriptive accounts of the purpose of life remain keenly intact and be given free reign and wide application. Indeed, I believe that both apply fully to every part of every human life at all times. The *vita receptiva* is a faithful expression of true sabbath-keeping, teaching us how to live continually in God's rest while we worship and while we work. Embracing the *vita receptiva* as the best understanding of the Christian's life allows both work as part of human ontology and leisure as the human telos to function fully and freely together as God intended. And what God intended is what he himself had put into place, decreed to be very good, and then delighted in at the completion of this world's first week of existence.

The time has come, then, to pull together all three threads of this book and bring the subject of chapter 2, the meaning of sabbath, directly into this discussion of the relationship between work and leisure. When considered together, it becomes clear that work, leisure, and sabbath are intricately and thoroughly interrelated in a complementary way that beautifully expresses, norms, and directs the shape and direction of human life. There is no conflict or contradiction between them. Woven together according to God's design, the resultant rope—or, in nautical terms, *line*—provides a direct, comprehensive, universal, and beautiful answer to the question of the purpose and meaning of human life. It is vital that we do more than merely conjecture, speculate, or postulate about man's purpose—brilliant as such philosophizing might be. Instead, the path we need to follow is to think about human life, its meaning and purpose, in terms of what actually comes to light through God's words and actions when he created the universe we inhabit together.

The narrative of creation reveals the plan that God intended for all his creatures when he designed and established the world—the world that he affirmed and celebrated on the seventh day of the world's first week. Understanding, appreciating, and adopting the scope and importance of what God did on that day as normative for every human life brings into crisp focus God's perfect answer to the nagging question at the core of every person's life—which demands an answer but that Western culture has abandoned as impossible to solve. Stymied by such an embarrassingly intractable question, serious Enlightenment thinkers like Huxley can only resort to trivializing the question as inconsequential. But the question is not irrelevant, and the answer is not a unicorn product of make-believe. Every person must ask the question, and God alone has the answer.

The answer to the meaning and purpose of life, and the resolution of the active and contemplative approaches to life, is the same. It is the sabbath. God's rest on the seventh day is the culmination and endorsement of creation. God's rest is not only the fulfillment of creation as a whole but also the telos of each individual creature whose purpose in life is to abide fully in God's rest, which is nothing more than God's approval and delight in his fully operational and wonderful creation. The telos of every man, woman, and child is the same. The meaning of our creation is to live in and with God as integral parts of his creation—in other words, to participate in God's rest, to celebrate sabbath with our Creator. Human work and human leisure are both indispensable and definitive aspects of God's plan for his creation because both are included in God's resting—his delighting-in, or sanctifying, or celebrating his creation.

Arriving at a rich and fully fledged understanding of sabbath means that we must be willing and able to abandon or at least enhance our rather flimsy, underdeveloped, and ultimately insubstantial and rather uninteresting ideas about sabbath as simply the negation of work, a solution to exhaustion, or the establishment of weekly prayer and worship attentive to the Word of God. Operating with an expansive understanding of sabbath as the fullness of every single member of creation interacting with God and with one another according to God's good plan is going to take some getting used to and will happen only after concerted effort. We have all learned to hear sabbath in the context of years of interpretation and teaching that are content with a severely abridged version of sabbath, hearing it only as divine approval of regular and substantial physical rest, as a somewhat arbitrary prohibition against any exertion, or as a command to go to church and pay attention. Generations of believers have been formed in the faith to think that sabbath-keeping matters for no other reason than that for some inexplicable reason it has been numbered among the Ten Commandments and so must be important for some reason. But that importance proves vapid and illusory when the commandment is all but exhausted simply by paying particular attention to one of the three standard options (don't work, take time to rest, go to church) or to some combination of the three.

Such a truncated view diminishes sabbath as a mere accoutrement for life, a reverential and pious embellishment, or a handy rule of thumb for optimal human productivity, or a means to proving unwavering obedience even to random rules. In these typical approaches, it is a struggle to find real significance for real life in our sabbath-keeping. This is why the effort to gain a truly robust and expansive view of sabbath grounded in God's seventh-day rest is at the same time absolutely essential and richly rewarding. Without it, people living in the Enlightened West will continue to struggle to solve the problem of meaning and purpose in life; but with it, those who know God's truth in

Christ not only will have hope for eternal life at the resurrection but will also come to understand the point of life in this world now. Understanding sabbath in terms of God's delight in his creation leads his people to see their own lives as the combination and integration of purposeful and prodigal investment of self for the sake of the other through their work, the heartfelt celebration and profound joy of genuine leisure in communion with God, and the delightful harmony between Creator and all creatures that should define and direct every part of every human life in this world.

Christians who live their lives with this way of thinking about sabbath not only live life as God intended but also provide the world around them with a compelling example of human being as it is supposed to be. They show the world that modern life is not a futile existence devoid of purpose, hopelessly aimless and obsessed with manufacturing meaning; but it is instead what God created it to be: a life sacrificially spending self for others through hard work, suffused with abiding wonder and awe in the goodness of God and his creation, and anticipating the perfect harmony of all creation, which is sampled even now in glimpses, sensations, melodies, tastes, and scents of a celebration already well along in its preparations. Nothing less than this is at stake in getting a right understanding of the interrelationship of sabbath, work, and leisure—in other words, a right understanding of the *vita receptiva*.

WHO'S RIGHT AND WHO'S WRONG?

Does this mean, then, that everyone with a thin, abbreviated, or one-dimensional view of the sabbath is wrong? No doubt my argument certainly seems to point in this direction. In fact, several years ago when I was first developing some of these ideas, I decided to try them out in their incipient form in a semipublic setting after a last-minute request to offer some teaching that might be interesting to a gathering of ecclesiastical leaders in the LCMS. I spent the time making the case as best I could for a robust and expansive view of sabbath along the lines of the argument I presented in chapter 2. It was directly after lunch, and the level of engagement and interaction wasn't the finest in my teaching career, but the deed was done, and I was on record with my rather unfamiliar take on sabbath. Before I could gather my iPad and notes from the podium, I was approached by one of the leaders of the leaders with a rather earnest question delivered unencumbered by surrounding comment but that he had generously decided to ask me in private. I don't remember the question verbatim, but it was something along the lines of, "So, are you saying that the explanation of the Third Commandment in Luther's Small Catechism is wrong?"

I should have seen it coming. I knew that the approach to sabbath that I was suggesting enlarged the significance and reach of the commandment significantly further than Luther's rather terse treatment. But I had been consumed with the scriptural case to be made and with the remarkable doctrinal matrix and marvelous implications that took shape when sabbath was granted its full meaning. But the fact remained that I was pushing beyond what Luther had deemed sufficient. I recall my response even less certainly than the question. Taken only a little off-guard by the minimally oblique suggestion that I was exhibiting less than stellar Lutheran orthodoxy, I think I indicated my disinclination ever to challenge the reformer, but then went on to acknowledge my departure from Luther, pointing, however, to his somewhat wider treatment in the Large Catechism—though as recognized previously, even this interpretation is still thin, content to limit the commandment to a body's need for rest and refreshment and the need to hear God's Word.

Having had a few years to think about all of this—and particularly that exchange—I think I'm ready now to attempt a more complete answer to what is certainly an appropriate question or series of questions. It is entirely fair to wonder whether indeed not only Luther but virtually everyone else in Christendom—from Luther and his successors focusing on tired bodies and hearing the Word, to Sabbatarians old and new intent on keeping the sabbath by assiduously avoiding whatever is deemed to qualify as work or at least treating the day differently from any other (and their number is legion), to those who disregard the command altogether as applicable only to Israel and irrelevant in light of the gospel—is wrong in what they teach about the sabbath. The answer is no, they are not all wrong . . . at least not entirely.

The last group holds the most problematic and, in my opinion, least faithful, position—but there is truth even here, as Christ explodes the sabbath's meaning well beyond the practice of his zealous Jewish contemporaries and wantonly tramples their petty sabbath legalisms. For their part, the Sabbatarians are right to see that the sabbath introduces a time and way of being that stands apart from ordinary ways of living. Sabbath time is special time. It deserves particular attention and sanctified, or set apart, ways of doing things. And, of course, Luther is certainly right to see a connection between sabbath-keeping and God's life-giving work through the Word creating, forgiving, sustaining, restoring, and sanctifying his people through the church's proclamation. Indeed, this connection puts him in good company with the author of Hebrews, who also closely correlated God's sabbath rest with the preaching of the Word. No less than three times in the space of twelve verses of Hebrews chapter 4, where God's enduring sabbath rest is celebrated and promised, the author likewise highlights the Word's proclamation—culminating in his famous designation of the Word of God as "sharper than any two-edged sword."[4] Luther certainly knew what he was doing when he penned his Small Catechism explanation of the Third Commandment. But I will also push a little further and harder and argue that when Luther focused his teaching on a right conception of the Christian life, an approach I think is perfectly captured as the *vita receptiva*, he was in truth teaching what amounts to a robust understanding of sabbath in spite of the obvious fact that his actual teaching about the sabbath was deliberately restrained for the reasons covered in chapter 1 above. Still, it's worth noting that even in his Word-focused treatment, Luther captures a significant sabbath element when he reminds catechumens that they are to attend to the Word "gladly." All of this is what I would answer today if confronted with the challenge: Was Luther's teaching on the Third Commandment wrong? It was certainly not wrong . . . but then neither did it say everything.

There is, it should be clear, more to the story—God's story, that is; and the narrative of Jesus and the attendant scriptural record of God's story of the world compel us to see the natural law core of the Third Commandment as more than each human being's self-evident need for physical rest or the essential importance of hearing God's Word, though this is obviously a vitally important truth.[5] The assorted standard interpretations of sabbath aren't necessarily wrong, but they don't go far enough.

4 Hebrews 4:12.

5 Yes, this point has been repeated almost ad nauseam, but it is repeated here yet again for the sake of reinforcing my essential agreement with Luther—and hopefully quelling all charges to the contrary.

They lack a comprehensive and foundational understanding of the place of God's rest and the corresponding commandment articulated at Sinai. They tend to become distracted by what they perceive to be abuses of the commandment—real or imagined—by legalisms (which are, no doubt, altogether real abuses of the commandment), or by an eager zeal to tap into what they are convinced is an almost magical blessing dispensed automatically by God when work is foresworn and regular routines set aside each seventh day in pious obedience to an ancient but very rarely understood command.

There are reasons, then, some good and some less than good, for Christians to settle for sabbath understandings that fall short of the full account grounded in God's actual words and actions. Nevertheless, whatever the reasons and however orthodox and useful the standard applications might be, there is no reason that the full sabbath picture—grounded in the creation, reaffirmed throughout the teaching and healing ministry of Jesus, and one day brought to fulfillment at the promised eschatological consummation—should be ignored or resisted by Christians. God's rest, established in the sabbath as taught in Scripture, and as I have attempted to present it here, provides a critical answer for our world today. It must be understood, taken to heart, and taught among Christians and then to the world.

In an effort to make my case as convincingly as I can, and cognizant—as noted—of the significant inertia in the church's thinking and teaching to handle the sabbath in familiar but inadequate ways, I will devote the second half of this lengthy chapter to fleshing out some of the immediate applications of a full understanding of the sabbath, particularly with regard to both work and leisure. Sabbath is not a restrictive mandate reining in human work or activity. Sabbath is not limited to one day each week for spiritual and physical rejuvenation. Sabbath is not exactly an attitude or mindset. Sabbath is a way of thinking about and acting on all that it means to be a human being. Sabbath is God's way for the world to exist, and so it is the telos of all created life. Sabbath is the fullness of God's plan for his creation brought to rich completion and celebrated. Sabbath makes plain the meaning and purpose of life. Sabbath is the *vita receptiva*. Sabbath is nothing less than the foundation and culmination of the world. And not only all of that but sabbath also resolves the impasse between work and leisure.

LIVING IN SYNC

The full argument for leisure as scholia was presented in the previous chapter. There I followed Josef Pieper contending that scholia, or intentional contemplation, should be understood as the fulfillment of man's guiding telos to live in harmony with God and with the surrounding creation and that this scholia, or leisure, is best and rightly celebrated in festivals rooted in worship. I won't rehearse it all again here; but it is worth pointing out explicitly that everything emphasized in relation to a classic understanding of leisure as the objective of human life correlates seamlessly with the rich and comprehensive biblical portrait of sabbath. God's seventh-day delight in his creation and the inclusion of Adam and Eve—the forebears and representatives of all humanity—in this celebration exemplifies the very core of true leisure. Leisure is not doing nothing, recharging, or entertainment. Leisure is living aware of the glory of God and the rich wonders of his creation, then recognizing and enhancing the harmony between and among Creator and all creatures that God built into the creation and that still endures throughout the creation, although sadly and painfully muted, strained, and obscured by the intrusion of sin and its curses. Leisure is closely akin to the rich understanding of sabbath as celebration that should not, indeed that *cannot*, be constrained or contained within a single day each week. Like sabbath, leisure should be understood as an accurate description of the target that aims and explains human existence.

In our zeal to align leisure with sabbath, however, we need to be careful to emphasize that true leisure is not just aimed upward toward union and communion with God. Leisure is not an exclusively vertical or only *coram Deo* goal. One does not contemplate and commune with God alone but with God and all creatures. Leisure means living in harmony with God and with all that he has made, especially fellow bearers of God's image. The same truth holds as we learn to keep sabbath. Sabbath is not just about God but about God along with the world he made. The Third Commandment has its roots in God's seventh-day rest and God's exodus rescue. In Genesis, God created the world and declared it very good. In Exodus, he worked to move forward his plan to redeem the world, saving Israel through whom he would then save all the world. This means that keeping sabbath is really nothing more than learning to receive and keep God's rest, which is simply God reveling in every part of his entire creation. So, the Third Commandment is concerned with much more than just a human being's vertical relationship with God. The Third Commandment is also focused on that person's relationships and interactions with all the creatures that God has placed around him in this world. Sabbath rest is all about delighting in what it means to be God's creature living in sync with God and with other creatures.

All of this is to say that contrary to the standard catechetical distinctions made when the commandments are typically introduced and taught, the Third Commandment is not best understood as a first table, God-centered commandment. In fact, thinking in terms of two tables of the law, one concerned with God (the first three or four commandments, depending on one's numbering) and the second directed toward other creatures (all the rest starting with the command to obey parents), usually adds more confusion than clarity to the way we understand the commandments. All ten are about what it means to be human as God intended. Keeping all ten commandments helps better form us into humans who bring honor to God and are of service to our neighbors. All ten, then, are for the benefit of the neighbor, even the first two—a Christian who worships God and honors his name either convicts those who see him worshiping God or encourages them to do the same; either way, the neighbor is served. In the case of the Third Commandment, the connection to other creatures is particularly compelling. Keeping sabbath is done not for the benefit of God nor even as a mark of personal piety and obedience. No, people are to keep the sabbath because doing so helps make each of us the kind of human God intended us to be: one who is a benefit to other creatures.

The sabbath is kept not for the sake of God nor for the sake of the one obeying the command. As with all the other nine commandments, the sabbath is kept for the sake of fellow creatures in the world. The law of God is the will of God for the right functioning of his creation. Keeping the commandments helps keep the world operating as intended. The commandment to keep the sabbath specifically serves the entire creation by providing a solid purpose and telos for each person that directs her to engage in life with an eye to the wholeness of creation and with the desire to cultivate greater connections and interactions with other members of creation as well as with the Creator.

And when this happens, life on earth is better for all involved because it better reflects God's plan. This means that rightly understanding and keeping sabbath is foundational for life that is properly oriented and lived in the world. In other words, we are better humans and better neighbors to those around us—and not just because we are well rested and have been encouraged by a recent trip to church. No, we are better humans because we understand the meaning of God's rest and what it means to keep sabbath. We know why we are here and what the point of our lives is all about. We are here to live in harmony with God and his will, to seek to live rightly with all the other creatures God has placed around us, and to treasure and celebrate this smooth functioning of the world in sync with God's plan. This is leisure. This is sabbath. This is what it means to be human according to God's plan.

This celebration of sabbath absolutely happens in divine worship—or it should. People coming together to consider God's grace and glory and to encourage one another in their worship of God and in following God's will for life is the very essence of contemplation, or scholia, or leisure. But keeping the sabbath also occurs when friends who share a common confession about the meaning and purpose of the world get together to enjoy a meal; play a few games in the yard or around a table; share conversation about things trivial and things poignant and painful; laugh out loud at inside jokes, at themselves, and at the sheer joy of being God's creatures in a dynamic relation with God and with one another; and simply relish what it means to be humans participating in God's good creation while anticipating the day of re-creation, restoration, and complete consummation of God's eternal plan. And keeping sabbath also happens when a husband and wife share their ten thousandth day together without even noticing the significance of the event but simply delighting in another day filled with the mundane delights of life together within God's plan for man and woman in the bond of marriage, not perfect but grace-filled and joyful. And keeping sabbath happens when standing seemingly alone on the shore of a lake of exquisitely flat water guarded behind by towering pines, maples, and birch and in front by the morning mists obscuring the far shore and hearing from somewhere surprisingly near the mesmerizing call of a loon—so still, so powerful, so brimming with the wonder of God's creative power. All of these are what it means to keep sabbath. Rightly considered and increasingly appreciated, all of these capture the meaning of human life—life in sync.

But this understanding of sabbath-keeping does not exhaust the meaning of God's rest or his subsequent command for us to observe our own sabbath rest. Indeed, incredible, and even absurd, as it may sound, I believe that our human work not only belongs as an essential part of our humanity but that, since sabbath captures the fullness of what it means to be God's human creature, work must also belong to our right keeping of sabbath.

LIVING IN SERVICE

Though I know only a handful by heart, I have to admit that I've long had a weakness for pithy French phrases. For me, there is something compelling about the sound of the Gallic language making a wry observation about life. A recent addition to my short list comes from Jean-Paul Sartre, one of the twentieth-century spokesmen for existentialism and the centrality of the individual self. He once declared, "*L'enfer, c'est les autres*—hell is other people."[6] While severe introverts might at

6 Jean-Paul Sartre, *No Exit and Three Other Plays* (New York: Vintage Books, 1946), 47.

times be inclined to agree with the sentiment, and earnest existentialists can capably defend the premise, most "nice" people will no doubt find the idea unsettling if not appalling. Very few people are willing to own the label of misanthrope. We like to imagine that we are open and generous toward others and that "of course, other people are important." It's a given: caring about other people is just part of basic human decency. Yet, the reality of life in the twenty-first century is that even if the other is not exactly hell, he is certainly not a central or even necessary component of the meaning of life. In our world, the self has emerged triumphant over all else. For the postmodern person—a designation not chosen but inflicted by virtue of the circumstances of birth, and so the default reality for virtually all people living in the West today—the individual self is at the center of everything. The self is lord and telos, displacing nation, community, church, neighbor, and even family as the core, object, and source of meaning in life. In our contemporary world, the other is at best a tool to be used for the benefit of the self's pursuit of fulfillment. In direct contradiction of Kant's categorical imperative, other people are knocked from their hallowed spot as ends and become nothing more than means.

While a world in which whatever one does is the result of calculations that are rarely conscious and deliberate and yet are unwaveringly and effectively aimed at advancing one's own agenda and enhancing one's own existence is our contemporary reality, it is certainly not the Christian way of life. Recalling once again Luther's concise summation of the Christian ethos underscores the very different way of living that should be the norm for God's people: "A Christian lives not in himself, but in Christ and in his neighbor. . . . By faith he is caught up beyond himself into God. By love he descends beneath himself into his neighbor."[7] When I was in college, a popular acronym had a way of appearing far too often in student-led devotions and Bible studies: J.O.Y., for Jesus, Others, Yourself. Living life with this order of priorities—Jesus first, others second, and self third—we were exhorted, was the path to true joy. But Luther's wisdom as articulated in his extraordinary prose leads us in a very different direction.

Luther rightly declares that Christians live entirely by faith in Christ. In other words, they are each made whole, complete, and fully saved only by trusting God's gift of forgiveness, freely delivered through faith in Jesus Christ. Faith is God's gift that receives God's grace. It is never a matter of human works. Saved only by grace, Christians are then sent back into God's world to do what God created and now redeemed them to do. And since by grace through faith in Christ they are completely right with God and their eternal salvation is covered, they are now free to devote 100 percent of their energies and attention to the work they've been given to do for the sake of their fellow creatures. In other words, they have twenty-four hours each day and seven days each week to do nothing but live their lives for the benefit of their neighbors. In a very real sense, the neighbor actually comes in first place on the list of our priorities since we humans are called to serve our neighbors first. It's important to remember that neither the Father nor the Son nor the Holy Spirit needs any human's service or anything else that any human has to offer. In our relationship with God, we don't give or offer anything but humble thanks and unbridled praise (and while this is the obligation of every creature, God doesn't *need* even this from us); before God, humans simply receive what only Jesus can give.

7 *Luther's Works*, 31:371.

Still, it is the third part of the old acronym, the "Yourself" part, that is actually the most misguided and problematic. While the J.O.Y. acronym has the "self" taking third place with the bronze medal, Luther allocates no space for the "Y" at all. For Luther, the self simply does not count. The self fails to make the list. Luther gets the dynamic, life-creating, self-denying truth of the Christian life exactly right. We receive from Jesus, then we live for others, and the self does not matter. In fact, the Christian dies to self; that's why he lives *outside* himself: in faith toward God—receiving what God gives and in love toward neighbor—giving whatever the neighbor needs. The self is not the center but exists as God intended, receiving both God's grace and God's purpose. And the purpose of God is crystal clear from Jesus' teaching and then throughout the pages of the Bible: serve the neighbor and live for the sake of the other. The only appropriate calculation a Christian should make, with regard to self, is to take care to be a faithful steward of his own mental, physical, emotional, and spiritual resources so that he will be ready and able to serve the neighbor well for as long as God grants life. That is to say that from a Christian standpoint, any and all self-care is done strictly for the benefit of others. It has the aim of making the self a capable servant to others for as long as possible. The Christian lives to serve the creation.

Recognizing the centrality of work for human being, and particularly for Christian life and witness, was the burden of chapter 3, where I argued that it is right to see work as part of our human ontology. In other words, work should be understood as a fundamental aspect of our humanity—we are born and redeemed to work. So, how does this idea fit with the argument of chapter 4 that man is made to live in contemplation, or leisure, or scholia? It fits by seeing work in a sabbath light. Which is not quite as paradoxical or contradictory as it may seem at first blush. God rested on the first seventh day and delighted in his creation—a creation which from the beginning included man as the lord and steward of creation, divinely given tasks which could be fulfilled only by doing work. This means that the creation celebrated by God on the seventh day was designed around man as worker. Man's work for the sake of the encompassing creation was always the plan. Work, then, is not antithetical to the seventh-day rest of God; in fact, human work is an essential aspect of all that God declared to be very good. Work is part of God's plan for man.

Serving the neighbor, the other, was never intended as a burden to be endured but was the whole point of human life and so was rightly received as a gift from God. That wonderful arrangement was shattered and disastrously distorted by sin, of course; after the fall, nothing is quite as it was supposed to be. In the brokenness of the world made demonic and evil by human rebellion and sin, the other who was to be the object and beneficiary of our work can indeed become a living incarnation of hell who injects pain, sorrow, difficulty, and weariness into our lives. Maybe Sartre wasn't quite as off base as it might have seemed. But it bears remembering that sin infects us all, and there is hell enough to go around, so that in this cursed world even we ourselves end up being another's hell. Smugness that names the other "hell" is only thinly veiled self-deception. But Jesus beats both sin and hell. Jesus puts humans back into right relationships with their Creator and with their fellow creatures. Jesus leads his people to live in the wonder and beauty of the receptive life, the down and out life: in faith down from God and in love out toward neighbor. And all of this is living according to God's plan, according to his design for the world, the design he celebrated on the seventh day. So it is that work is not the polar opposite of sabbath. Quite the contrary, it is an essential component of sabbath. That's why, as I argued in chapter 3, even at the eschaton when all is made whole and complete, the creation is brought to the breathtaking pinnacle of God's eternal plan, and humanity is at last all that humans were always created to be, humans, you and I, will be working for the sake of the creation and to the glory of God. We'll be working in a sabbath way—the ultimate sabbath way, in harmony with God's plan.

Doing work in a sabbath way does not mean doing it in a slow-paced or laid-back way. It does not mean finding work that is not overly taxing or demanding, or that can perhaps be done without breaking a sweat or breaking one's brain. In fact, any and all attempts to mitigate or soften the blow of work for the sake of self always lead in directions away from sabbath. They are opposed to sabbath work because they aim at self-preservation. The point of true sabbath work is that it is always aimed out and done for the sake of the other. The Good Samaritan did what his neighbor needed. It was work. It was good work. It was sabbath work. Jesus, who is the ultimate Good Samaritan, did hard work. It seemed to exhaust him—well, Jesus as fully human was routinely exhausted because Jesus as fully God was doing what God routinely did: divine work. It was sabbath work, and so unsurprisingly, as detailed in chapter 2, it seemed to fall in particular on sabbaths.

> The man went away, and told the Jews that it was Jesus who had made him well. For this reason the Jews were persecuting Jesus, because He was doing these things on the Sabbath. But He answered them, "My Father is working until now, and I Myself am working."[8]

8 John 5:15–17.

Working. God the Father is working. God the Son is working. God is working to care for his creation. He is redeeming his creation, healing what is broken, restoring what is out of place, reclaiming what had been lost to sin and hell. For the sake of the creation that he loves, God works. He works himself to death. This is sabbath work. This is the good of the neighbor being served regardless the price to self.

Human work done for the other, done in the context of the vocations that come to us as tasks and as gifts from God, is sabbath work. Sabbath is not the abolition of work but the context and fulfillment of work. When sabbath is rightly understood as the observation of God's rest, God's celebration of the creation, it is evident not only that sabbath has room for work but that work is an essential aspect of sabbath. We work to serve the other and to aid the celebration of God's extraordinary creation. Remembering that leisure and festival and worship are all tightly bound to one another, we realize that work must attend even leisure, or no festival or worship could ever move past a mere idea and come to fruition in lived reality. Indeed, the best festivals take a great deal of work, but it is work done for the sake of leisure, for the sake of the other, for the sake of sabbath. It is true and good and beautiful work. A schedule is prepared, places are cleaned, food is planned and crafted, sermons are written and studied, music is arranged and practiced, games are organized, tables are set, bonfires and fireworks are readied. Work. It is all a great deal of work. And it is all in and part of the celebration of festival. It is all an integral part of sabbath as God intended, sabbath as something far greater than the mere absence of labor.

Sabbath work is not an oxymoron; it is the very crux and nexus of what contemplation (or leisure or scholia), vocation (or human work for the sake of the other), and sabbath (or

God's seventh-day rest) are all meant to accomplish. Together they define and direct human being and life. Together they make life matter. They give our human existence purpose that extends even beyond our short time in this broken yet redeemed world that is on its way to restoration and glory. And it is God's people—God's stewards of creation, who celebrate sabbath with God and with one another, who receive what God gives, and who in turn serve those around—whom God places at the head of the resurrection procession to his eternal kingdom.

DOING THE VOCATION THAT NEEDS TO BE DONE

The idea of sabbath work is undoubtedly the hardest new idea that I'm asking the reader to consider. So, rather than offering support for sabbath work with illustrative vignettes that spring from my own imagination or experience, I'll let a handful of compelling selections from literature do that work. It should be noted that none of these authors mentions the idea of sabbath in the chosen selections, and none of them should be assumed as advocates of my understanding of sabbath work. In fact, it's entirely possible that each one would reject my argument outright—I'm not intending to implicate them. However, laying claim to the very real power of art to communicate truth, goodness, and beauty that may never have occurred to the author, I believe that each of these selections offers a potent picture of what work can become in the context of sabbath as God's rest.

The first offering comes from Leo Tolstoy's *Anna Karenina* and recounts the experience of Levin, a landowner, who voluntarily, indeed eagerly, spends a day mowing grass with the peasants who labor on his estate. The work is demanding as, armed with their scythes, the mowers form a phalanx that then progresses with steady strokes through fields and pastures as the workers cut the grass with long swings of the blades that are freshly sharpened during every short break. Levin works for the sheer joy of the physical labor and, it seems, to prove to himself his own ability to accomplish the work that most noblemen would eschew as plebeian and unnecessarily wearisome. For Levin, the delight is in the very work itself. As he shares life in the field with his workers for a day, he becomes a guest participant in their routine—the ritual of mowing that is constructed of words, actions, skills, perceptions, and personal interactions that are all woven into the life of the earthbound peasants. Levin does not work because he must but for the sake of the work itself and for the bonds that it reaffirms not only between himself and those who labor on his land but between himself and the land itself. He yearns for the labor, that he might be an intimate part of the essential work done for the sake of the creation.

Tolstoy's account is a delight to read in full, but perhaps to whet an appetite for outstanding literature, a couple passages will serve to capture the beauty of the prose and the power of work for Levin:

> Levin went down his own swath in the same way, then—in spite of the perspiration that ran down his face in streams and dripped from his nose and though his back was as wet as if the shirt had been soaked in water—he felt very light-hearted. . . .
>
> They came to the end of another swath. They went on mowing long and short rows, good and poor grass. Levin had lost all count of time and had really no idea whether it was late or early. His

> work was undergoing a change which gave him intense pleasure. While working he sometimes forgot for some minutes what he was about, and felt quite at ease; then his mowing was nearly as even as that of Titus. . . .
>
> The longer Levin went on mowing, the oftener he experienced those moments of oblivion when his arms no longer seemed to swing the scythe, but the scythe itself his whole body, so conscious and full of life; and as if by magic, regularly and definitely without a thought being given to it, the work accomplished itself of its own accord. There were blessed moments.[9]

My guess is that most readers can readily identify with Levin's experience in the field. Not that we all know the peculiar trials and joys of agricultural work firsthand—in truth, in our world people with such bona fide experiences are increasingly rare. Still, I suspect that the singular sensation of utterly losing oneself in work is not so uncommon. Not only hard physical work but even rigorous mental effort can become so thoroughly consuming that all else fades into nonexistence and the task itself becomes the only reality. On those occasions, time is irrelevant, progress on the work is the only measure that matters, and when the work is overwhelmingly engrossing as it was for Levin, it is at once absolutely exhausting and incomparably wonderful.

9 Leo Tolstoy, *Anna Karenina*, in Gilbert Meilaender, ed., *Working: Its Meaning and Its Limits* (Notre Dame: University of Notre Dame, 2000), 33, 34, 35.

Levin's work was sabbath work, not only because he did it willingly and with zeal and joy but because it was work done in harmony with his own being and with other creatures—not only fellow humans but also the grass and the earth and the air and the rain and even the scythe. Levin was in tune with it all and doing work for the good of all, helping to lay up a store against the coming winter.

Jumping a century and a hemisphere away, we move from Tolstoy's nineteenth-century Russia to Wendell Berry's twentieth-century Kentucky and meet his quintessential farmer, Elton Penn. Elton, though, is not like Levin. Elton does not work by choice but by necessity. And Elton does not relish and anticipate his work—quite the opposite:

> When he had the work still ahead of him, there would always come a time when he dreaded it. The tobacco harvest always came upon him that way, and followed the same course, at once surprising and familiar, from seeming impossibility to obvious possibility to eventual completion, when almost strangely the great effort would be behind him, and he would become again far-sighted in his thoughts desiring the coming year.[10]

Because Elton lives in a community of farmers, there is a responsibility and obligation that urges him forward, one that is shared by all the farmers who live life together working on one another's farms during the busiest times of harvest. And while Berry crafts a story in which Elton spends his day alone,

10 Wendell Berry, "A Friend of Mine" in *That Distant Land* (Washington, DC: Counterpoint Press, 2004), 322.

memorably accomplishing the feat of single-handedly cutting and spearing four rows of the large, yellow tobacco leaves, he works the entire time aware and in concert with all the other members of his community. As Elton warms to the task and finds the rhythm and stride of his own work, he finishes the first row, and the description of the work, then, is altogether reminiscent of Levin:

> He had rested for no more than five minutes, and now he went back to his work before its momentum left him. The dread was long past. He did not even remember it. He liked where he was and what he was doing. He had fallen, there on the Rowanberry place, into a happiness he recognized as Art Rowanberry's: feeling good and satisfied with what he had. . . .
>
> He was in it now. It was as though his motion through the field was not made by him, but he by it, and it was carrying him. It would carry him to the row's end, and to the end of the next and the next, to the day's end, and then it would release him to his rest. And yet there was a momentum that went beyond tiredness and sleep. It would carry him on and on, through the fall days and into the cold, and into the spring again, and on to other years. He could feel it moving in him like the flow of blood, and through him like a wind.[11]

11 Ibid., 324, 325.

Elton is doing sabbath work. Yes, it begins reluctantly and without desire—without even the remotest hint of sabbath. Yet in spite of his own misgivings and resistance, Elton falls into sabbath work. Taught by the community that raised and formed him, he works with the land and the tools and in harmony with the creation for the sake of the creatures around him. No doubt, we could call for and initiate a lively and probably acrimonious discussion about the evils of tobacco and question the degree of good Elton was actually doing for his neighbor, but to do so would miss the point altogether. It would allow the demonic inbreaking and perversion of sin that corrodes and spoils the very fabric of all creation, including man's labor, to steal from us the divine truth and reality that always undergirds and supports—and on special occasion, blatantly breaks through into human awareness—even the most arduous and sometimes morally dubious human work. Although human sin too often perverts God's good plan, the work that God gives us to do for the sake of the other remains sabbath work. The point not to be missed here is that vocation is not the enemy of leisure but its complement. Work is not the contradiction of sabbath but its essential component.

Finally, a discussion of sabbath work would not be complete without a consideration of J. R. R. Tolkien's marvelous little story "Leaf by Niggle." If appreciation of Berry's story requires the suspension of some exacting ethical criteria, benefiting from Tolkien's account of Niggle's unremarkable life, death, restoration, and eventual remarkable work in the eternal kingdom requires suspension of a few doctrinal criteria related to purgatory. One cannot offer a blanket endorsement of the story of Niggle's journey. Nevertheless, there is power in Tolkien's story and truth for us to glean, because he so intricately links the events, the plans, the aspirations, the work, and the actual accomplishments and failures of this life to the altogether physical and vivid realities of the next life. The masterwork of Niggle's life—a magnificent canvas on which he has painted a tree crowned with an exquisite canopy of leaves, each one a masterpiece of intricate detail—is, after Niggle's death, pressed into service to patch the roof of his neighbor, Parish, a neighbor for whom Niggle had often done errands and acts of kindness out of a sense of compulsion with a very poor attitude indeed. But, in the life after death, in the new heavens and the new earth, Niggle discovers the continuity and the fullness of the work that had occupied his days in the sin-corrupted world.

As Tolkien unfolds his protagonist's not entirely pleasant experiences after death, Niggle at last finds himself in a world of sunshine, springtime, hills, gates, grass, and bicycles—the very things that had comprised his previous life. In fact, the extraordinary land through which he rides his bicycle is altogether familiar to him. Cruising through his new world, he suddenly stops short, literally falling off his bicycle under the shadow of an enormous, perfect tree: his tree. The tree he had created through countless hours of long, loving labor now moves and grows and lives in the midst of this new creation. Marveling at the wonder before him, Niggle's arms raise in gratitude and praise, and he declares aloud the truth that what he now beholds, both his work of art and also its fulfillment, is a gift. With his delightful prose (a taste of which, were it not for stifling copyright restrictions, I would have eagerly shared), Tolkien suggests a powerful truth. It is a marvelous thought that in God's economy nothing is lost, and that our meager efforts are taken up into God's perfect plan and made into what is truly spectacular and indeed a gift to all of creation.

Yet, the most intriguing aspect of Tolkien's picture of the new creation is the inclusion and heightening of human relationships. In time, Parish also arrives in Niggle's corner of the new creation, and the two neighbors finally meet again. Like old roommates, not needing even to speak, they simply acknowledge one another with a nod and then set to work together. Surveying their corner of the new creation, they concur on the right place to build a small house and its garden. With their tools and skills, they accomplish together their plans—Niggle actually now the more focused on the task of building and gardening and the newly made Parish more inclined to stroll through the land gazing at the trees, and most particularly *the* tree, Niggle's masterwork. Neighbors in the former temporal life, the two men now become co-laborers in God's re-created world. The neighbor who had been an intrusive hell for poor Niggle when he only wanted to paint now became the partner in his true work, the true work of humanity, tending God's creation.

The work and the relationships of this life, even when superficial or inadequately accomplished, become in God's new creation wonderful gifts and the means of still greater works. In this world, grudgingly and distractedly, yet willingly and for the sake of the other, Niggle had done sabbath work as he served Parish and others around him. In the Kingdom after death, he was continuing his sabbath work but in an entirely new dimension and with far greater joy and delight. The continuity of human work done for the benefit of the creation, for the good of the neighbor, is the heart of sabbath work. Sabbath work is worship of God every bit as much as contemplation and leisure are worship of God. Both leisure and work are bound together in the reality of God's plan for his creation celebrated as sabbath. There is nothing at all contradictory about sabbath work; work and sabbath belong together always and fully.

THE MEANING THAT IS THERE

God created all that is, for the sheer delight of creating. The universe does not accomplish some necessary purpose or satisfy some divine need—God has no need of anything. Yet, what came into existence as an arbitrary action of God is for us who inhabit this world now shot through with the meaning that God gives to it. There is meaning, and man does have purpose. We live to accomplish God's plan. We live to care for the creation and so to honor God. We live to delight in the creation and so to honor God. We live to celebrate sabbath with our Creator and all of the surrounding creation. Leisure is the telos of man, and work is wired into his very being, and together they bring man into the rest of God, the practice of true sabbath. That God has actually, fully, and eternally joined himself to the creation in the incarnation brings another startling dimension to the significance and meaning of creation—but more fully pursuing the Christological component of the meaning of creation will have to be the work of another project. For now, filling out and amplifying the understanding of sabbath and relating it to both leisure and vocation is work enough. And, if the ideas brought together in this chapter are even partly grasped and applied, the potential positive impact on real lives is significant.

People living in the world of the Enlightened West are desperate for the meaning and purpose that the church has in abundance and is commanded to share. All people need to learn the beauty and joy that come with the *vita receptiva*. They will learn it only when they see it in action, when they see it in the lives of Levins and Eltons and Niggles who live next to them and who serve them according to the vocations that God gives, delighting in the wonder of God's creation and celebrating sabbath as the expansive and unsurpassable rest of God. This is the sabbath work of God's people.

CHAPTER 6

SLEEP AND PLAY

For a book that promised to be about your life, there is a great deal that has been ignored. There have been no extended discussions or intentional exploration of family and marriage, of sexuality, of food and eating, or of relationships with friends and enemies in neighborhoods or at work. I have not even mentioned the place of hobbies, avenues of amusement, or vacations. All of these topics make up, in varying gradations of importance, aspects of your life that matter. Nevertheless, as you can guess by the number of pages that remain, I am going to address none of these topics—significant and fascinating as they may be—and will leave them for others to cover. In fact, all of these topics have already been explored countless times over for many years now in diverse ways, including doctrinally and spiritually, by a plethora of authors with varying degrees of success. There are, though, two more life-defining topics directly related to the particular interests of this book—work, leisure, and sabbath—that are not often or extensively considered or discussed from a theological point of view and that deserve some attention—especially in the context of sabbath rest. In this chapter, then, I will address the separate topics of play and sleep and reflect in an introductory manner on the ways that each of these significant aspects of human existence relate to the shape of our lives. Play is also an important topic for consideration since it serves as an appropriate term to describe what we used to call *leisure* before we followed Josef Pieper in restoring a much richer and fuller meaning to that word. The sort of activity that we once labeled leisure, as the rest of the world continues to do, fits perfectly under the term *play*.

IS IT WORK OR IS IT PLAY?

When the starting shortstop for any of the thirty Major League Baseball teams goes to the ballpark on game day, is he going there to play or to work? The fact that he is likely earning tens of thousands of dollars to play that single game more than qualifies him as a professional athlete—though his agent is likely to insist that his professional status deserves to be appreciated and financially recognized still more. Even if a big leaguer never achieves elite superstar status that will land him in Cooperstown, and regardless the inevitable complaints, there is not a starting position player in MLB who is not being very well compensated for his time on the field. Naturally, his compensation takes into account the investment of an entire life, as every game day is preceded and surrounded by an enormous amount of time and energy committed to practicing and preparing for success on the field. And players will take their preparation exceedingly seriously. But it is still just a game, right? And if it is a game, then the players play, don't they? Or, is it possible that for these players baseball has, in fact, become nothing but work, the element of play all but snuffed out long ago and now only a distant memory of a time lost in the past when it really was just love of the game that was the only motivation? Can one meaningfully talk about a *work* ethic of *play*ers? On the face of it, this conjunction of words seems entirely inappropriate, but we are so accustomed to such ways of talking that we hardly notice the oddity.

The fuzzy distinction between work and play is nicely showcased by sports stars, but professional athletes do not provide the only example of the line between play and work being difficult to discern. Even those who never confuse their work with play, who know their work strictly and only as work, may nevertheless experience the confusion for themselves when it comes to the effort and work they willingly invest in chosen pastimes or "fun" pursuits, whether that be golf or gardening or grilling or even garbage recycling. There are very few hobbies or activities—no matter how rudimentary or simple—that do not rapidly expand and evolve upward into enormously complicated endeavors with their own idiosyncratic experts, authorities, skills, tools, ethos, organizations, and websites that characterize and codify the "right" way to engage in the chosen activity. A few web searches of any randomly selected topics you can imagine will prove my point.[1] Even simple hobbies quickly become demanding tasks with protocols, newsletters, conventions, and established standards to guide one's progress into that selected world of interest—and achieving a measure of success in the field inevitably comes with an exponentially increasing price tag attached. A toy designed for fun like a Frisbee or yo-yo, or a game meant to be merely amusing like hopscotch or Monopoly, can become an avocation, a pursuit, an obsession, a challenge, a burden. The border between chosen pursuit and exacting and expensive obsession is often blurry.

The tendency to obscure the distinctions between work and play is not new. Already in the late nineteenth century, one of the American humorists, a unique breed of writer that seemed to be a fitting product of that era, made the wry observation about his countrymen that has since achieved all but cliché status: "We worship our work. We work at our play. And we play at our worship."[2] The world described in the quote, a world of total work facilitated by times of refreshing recuperation with

1 If you doubt me, or lack imagination, try starting with "stick collector" or "stone skipping."

2 Gordon Dahl, *Work, Play, and Worship in a Leisure-Oriented Society* (Minneapolis: Augsburg, 1972), 20.

both centered on personal fulfillment, is quite familiar to us all. I sought to address some of the problems that stem from this idolization of work and instrumentalization of leisure already in chapters above. But the quote also highlights the more precise problem that is my present concern: the interface between work and play. If we often work at our play, and I suspect that few would disagree with this observation, and if on occasion our work actually seems like play, then how do we figure out where one ends and the other begins?

In fact, a precise distinction between work and play is not quite so confounding or elusive as it is sometimes made to seem. The difference has nothing to do with the degree of time, effort, or financial investment involved. Nor is the distinction solved by determining the degree of pleasure or enjoyment attendant to an activity—I know people who find far more enjoyment in their work than in what they do in the name of play. And the difference between work and play has nothing to do with what compensation does or does not result from the activity; whether or not you get paid for doing it is not the sole criteria—though, as will become clear, if one does something for the purpose of financial gain, it is by definition work. What distinguishes work from play is ultimately the question of ends and objectives.

All work is aimed at a purpose beyond itself. Work has an objective, an end that one is seeking to achieve through the work. The work itself becomes instrumental, a tool to be used, toward that desired end. A man works in the yard to secure a pleasant microenvironment for his household and to sustain his neighborhood reputation sufficiently intact. He plants crops in order to feed his family. He works in a corporation for the same purpose, though perhaps with considerably more pleasurable embellishments available—all for the good of the family, of course. Work always serves a greater goal. Usually and obviously, the goal is financial gain; but monetary compensation is not the only criteria, as there are plenty of other worthy goals we can name that motivate our work. The point is that there is always some driving purpose on the other side of the work.

Play, on the other hand, has no purpose beyond itself. This is the definitive issue. While play may be entertaining or enjoyable or refreshing, none of those things are the determining factors of play. What makes play, play is that it has no instrumental value. It is not undertaken with an ulterior motive. A child does not play for any other reason than to play. That adults often try to "leverage" child's play into teachable moments only proves that parents don't understand play and are, in fact, often experts at destroying perfectly good play by injecting some bothersome lesson or another into the event. The fact that child's play, and adult play for that matter, actually does achieve significant goods in the way of physical, mental, emotional, moral, and social development is merely a delightful byproduct and happenstance that accompanies what is in reality an event that is its own end. And the moment someone tries to play in order to accomplish some greater purpose, that play has been destroyed as play and has morphed into work. Play is its own end and thus its own purpose. It cannot be instrumentalized or pressed into service for some greater end—or, at least, it *should* not be so perverted and ruined. When play is turned into a tool for some good beyond itself, it ceases to be play. The whole point of play is its lack of purpose.

Dietrich Bonhoeffer makes precisely this observation in his *Ethics*: "In its essential distance from all purposefulness, play is the clearest expression that bodily life is an end in itself."[3] In other words, purposeless does not mean worthless or

3 Dietrich Bonhoeffer, *Dietrich Bonhoeffer Works*, vol. 6, *Ethics*, ed. Clifford J. Green, trans. Reinhard Krauss, Charles C. West, and Douglas W. Stott (Minneapolis: Fortress Press, 2009), 187–88.

pointless—quite the opposite, in fact; it simply means that one cannot press the activity into the service of some other, greater outcome. Play in the context of human existence and being is its own purpose and needs no further justification. Work, on the other hand, is always aimed at accomplishing something for the sake of a greater end and is justified by the good outcome that is produced. Even when work is rightly acknowledged as an ontological foundation of what it means to be human, as I argued above, it still serves some greater end. It may be part of my very humanity, but I never do it for its own sake; I do it for the sake of getting something done. When one plays it is never to get something done. Adam was built to work; but his work had a purpose: he worked to care for the creation. His activity was work because it had an aim. So it is with MLB shortstops. Baseball players—at least at the level of the major leagues—are clearly working. They have a goal and purpose in their activity at the stadium that exceeds mere participation in a game that is its own end. Not only are ball players working for a paycheck with which to support their families (with a hefty addition of many very fine embellishments well beyond mere sustenance), they are also essential components in a complex industry that offers a product, or perhaps products, and generates a great deal of revenue for an enormous number of people who likewise are able to provide for their own families, albeit often with far fewer frills than those who own and manage the teams and play the games—a competent beer-man certainly benefits from, but enjoys far fewer financial rewards than, the shortstop.

Still, deciding that shortstops work doesn't settle the question entirely. It can't quite escape the inherent ambiguity present when a professional athlete plays a game. After all, the purpose of the player's work is ultimately the participation in and extension of what is finally nothing but a game, the essence of purposeless play. Even the product of the MLB industry (it should be noted that in the case of professional sports, one is compelled to use the terms *product* and *industry* very generously with the widest possible degree of latitude in the definitions) is in the end nothing more than entertainment, diversion, and a wealth of statistics and records to distract and beguile the truly committed fans among the millions who follow the sport with varying levels of loyalty and interest. People may speak and behave otherwise, but baseball is and always will be nothing but a game, and a game is the manifestation of play. And yet, baseball is a game that for hundreds of thousands of individuals is the source, or a significant contributing foundation, of their work. So, while a precise distinction between work and play is not so difficult or complicated—the former is purposeful, and the latter is purposeless—the interface between them, along with the live possibility that any given activity may move easily and quickly from one category to the other even for the same person, frequently makes the distinction between work and play difficult to discern in actual application.

It is helpful to keep in mind that the level of a person's particular enjoyment in an activity does not enter into the distinction between work and play. Tolstoy's landowner, Levin, who relished the chance to spend a day of hard labor mowing with his peasants, thoroughly enjoys every aspect of the experience. If it was part of his vocabulary, he might even be tempted to describe the day as fun. But having fun is not the same as play. Nor did his day qualify as play because he did it without the burden of compulsion. It may be true that work is often done out of necessity while play seldom rises to that level of urgency; nevertheless, indispensability is not the decisive standard that marks off work from play. And however Levin or we might be tempted to regard it otherwise, the Russian gentleman certainly did spend his day in the fields doing *work*. It was work because it was aimed at a definite purpose—get the grass cut so it can dry and be gathered into barns. Work is purposeful; play is purposeless—that is the criteria.

DOES IT EVEN MATTER?

Perhaps, though, trying to discern the precise distinction between work and play is a project that doesn't actually need to occupy that much of our time or attention. From an academic standpoint, it is probably interesting to distinguish precisely between work and play. But considered within the interests of this book and in real life, it may not actually matter that much whether or not we are able to categorize with precision what we are doing as either work or play. Indeed, overthinking the question and devoting more than a minute or two to analyzing a situation and then evaluating whether it qualifies as work or play is very likely to lead in an entirely wrong direction of self-absorbed introspection or legalistic self-justification. Living instead in a sabbath way that centers on God's rest and that learns the art of delighting in both the Creator and the creation leads us to understand our work as an integral and so true, good, and beautiful part of what it means to be human as we seek to serve the creation around us. In this light, it is entirely appropriate that work can be thoroughly enjoyed, and even be counted as fun—in fact, such an outlook would constitute the best possible attitude toward work. So, work done well and in tune with God's plans and direction—in other words, work done as sabbath work—can absolutely and rightly be a source of joy and even refreshment for a worker. That is as it should be. But being able to work in such a way does not mean, then, that the contented and joyful worker has thus transformed his work into play or eliminated the essential place of play from his life. Play is a worthy and, rightly understood, even a necessary pursuit in a rightly ordered human life. You might say it is a necessary purposeless endeavor.

Humans need to play not to fulfill some hidden commandment, meet some suppressed human craving, or allow time for personal recreation whether spiritual, mental, emotional, or physical. Play is important not for a manufactured instrumental value (by definition, if it is in any way instrumental, it ceases to be play) but for the very fact that it is purposeless and exists for its own sake. The great American sociologist Peter Berger even asserted that playful elements, which "can be found in just about any sector of human culture," are so important that "culture as such would be impossible without this dimension."[4] Play matters because it is the affirmation that we humans are not so essentially important or life so deadly serious that every human action must be justified as worthwhile and productive. Play matters not as the antithesis of work but as a reminder that there is more to human existence than only work. Indeed, Berger pushes the significance of play further yet and sees in play a connection to joy and to life beyond or outside of time:

> Joy is play's intention. When this intention is actually realized, in joyful play, the time structure of the playful universe takes on a very specific quality—namely, *it becomes eternity*.[5]

Berger goes on to explain that play's purposelessness and keeping of time outside of ordinary time bring or bump us into the orbit of the greater surrounding realities of transcendence

4 Peter Berger, *A Rumor of Angels: Modern Society and the Rediscovery of the Supernatural* (Garden City, NY: Anchor Books, 1970), 57–58.

5 Ibid., 58. Italics in original.

that undergird and bind our existence. When we are lost in play, the world around—with its very real pain, suffering, and death—is suspended for a time. Play acts as a sort of intrusion of eternity into this world.

> The experience of joyful play is not something that must be sought on some mystical margin of existence. It can be readily found in the reality of ordinary life. Yet within this experienced reality it constitutes a signal of transcendence, because its intrinsic intention points beyond itself and beyond man's "nature" to a "supernatural" justification.[6]

Christians should not hastily dismiss these ideas as mere philosophical or pagan musings with no ground in Christian confession. Berger is articulating truths about human existence that are wired into the fabric of creation itself, what we typically call natural-law truths. These truths will not reveal the gospel, nor will pursuing these truths bring one into union with God—neither of these things can ever happen apart from Christ. Yet, the truths at work in the world that God created are not negated by the fuller revelation that comes through the incarnate Christ; in Christ, the built-in truths are brought to their completion. The wise course is to recognize the continuity in God's revelation—incipient in the world and unveiled in the Son. That play, even the play of pagans, points to realities beyond this world is a truth that should be observed, embraced, and then exploited by Christians who seek to bring their fellow humans to live in the fullness of God's perfect revelation in Jesus Christ.

6 Ibid., 60.

It has been established that play is certainly not work, nor vice versa; but it also needs to be stressed that play is not a synonym for leisure, or scholia. Leisure aims at contemplative delight in the great truths of this universe. Leisure is the festive celebration of the Creator and his creation. Play, then, is related to, and may even be a part of, leisure broadly understood; but play does not carry the overtones of contemplation or reflective awareness of greater truths and realities. Quite the opposite, in fact: play is an occasion when what is seen is exactly what is and nothing more is to be sought. The game is the thing, or as Shakespeare put it, with all of his typical multilayered profundity keenly in mind and affirmed, "The play's the thing."[7] Play exists for itself, and we participate in play for its own sake—and for the sake of the human privilege of being capable of taking part. Understood this way, play is of paramount importance not only for children but for adults.

Thus, while we do not need to devote much to the task of distinguishing between work and play, we would be wise to attend to both of these critical aspects of our humanity and to allow each their fitting place in our lives. Work is integral to what it means to be human, and so is play. A life lived as God intends will find both present in appropriate measure. Not only does all work and no play make Jack a very dull boy, but it actually makes him a very poor human being. No formula or ratio of work to play is needed or even possible. The important thing is that time and energy is committed to both pursuits without a need for explanation or justification of either. And while for most of us work will outweigh, in both time and energies spent, the place of play in our lives, we must be careful not to let the significance or obvious instrumental value of our work lead us to spurn or disparage the great good of play in our lives.

7 *Hamlet*, Act 2, Scene 2.

An evening enjoying a favorite board game with friends is the essence of play: it is time outside normal time with rules and goals and a way of being that for a while suspends the way of life in the real world around. And an hour of pickleball, spontaneously engaged with a pair of opponents you know less by first names quickly forgotten than by the peculiarly fast reflexes of the one and an impressive slicing backhand of the other, is time well spent for the sheer purposelessness of the game itself. It is not the exercise, the camaraderie, the fresh air, or the sharpening of hand-eye coordination that justifies the game. It is the game and your part in it that justify the game. If you play well, so much the better. If you enjoy the play—as you should—better yet. But even if neither are true, the game and the play are still rightly done simply for the sake of having done them. And the game and the play enhance and enrich our very humanity by whispering truths of transcendence even when we are not listening.

THE PURSUIT OF PLAY

Christians who seek to live lives in tune with God's purposes, celebrating God's seventh-day rest and honoring the sabbath, will be committed to nurturing the place of play in their lives. So, yes, this is a call for deliberate, scheduled times of play for the simple sake of the play. It is a call for game nights and game libraries and for the carefree and careless dabbling in hobbies at which you do not excel. G. K. Chesterton, whose life bridged the transition from the nineteenth century into the twentieth and whose observations about those years are still richly and often uncannily applicable to our lives a century later, once famously, or perhaps infamously, quipped, "If a thing is worth doing, it is worth doing badly."[8] His sentiment has perplexed and confounded people ever since he wrote it, because it sounds so completely unorthodox in its utter rejection of what we were all taught in one form or another from our earliest years: "Be it great or be it small, do it well or not at all." Notwithstanding his apparent challenge to traditional moral training (which is indeed only apparent), I think Chesterton's axiom is wonderful. Yes, the rebel in me must admit an attraction simply because the dictum veers so wantonly out of the accepted groove of the expectation of continued refinement and improvement. But, perhaps the more accurate reason for my delight in Chesterton's idea is the hard truth that I excel at so very few athletic feats or games. I try, but I do not succeed. Practice does not always make perfect. Sometimes, maybe often, it merely reinforces mediocrity. So, Chesterton's idea resonates with me.

There is more to the axiom's point, though, than assuaging a non-athlete's lifelong frustration. To say that if a thing is worth doing, it is worth doing badly is not an excuse for poor effort, indifference, or contentment with failure. Chesterton's point is the very opposite. Things that are worth doing, like raising children to be followers of Christ and people of character and like being a good spouse, a conscientious homeowner, a decent typist, or a competent swimmer, bike rider, left fielder, or friend are worth doing by everyone. These are all things that matter—not all equally or to the same degree, of course, but they all matter and are all things that one should be able to do. And since everyone needs to do them, it is evident from what we know about the marked differences among humans that we will not all excel at all of them. "Jack of all trades and master

8 G. K. Chesterton, *What's Wrong with the World* (New York: Dodd, Mead and Company, 1910), 202.

of none" is not an indictment but an objective that should encourage all of us to continue to do things that are part of what it means to be human simply for their own sake and not because we may or may not be good at any given thing.

This is the glory of the amateur over the professional. The amateur plays softball on the church league not because he is an outstanding shortstop but because the team needs nine players to compete and he happens to have picked up a few things about fielding ground balls and learned to swing a bat with reasonable consistency. He plays because playing is good, not because he is good at playing. If we only do those things that we have a chance of one day reasonably mastering and conquering, then we live inadequate, thin, and rather bland lives that are frankly less than fully human lives. The Latin root of *amateur* is *amare*, "to love." Amateurs play for love of the game, with no other objective than playing. Professionals are forced to forsake the purity of play and instrumentalize it as a means to another end—the making of money usually at the head of the list. In a very real sense, then, those amateurs who do a thing badly do it far better than the virtuosos, savants, aficionados, and wizards who command the attention of the world. We rightly marvel at the expert's ability to do what we know we will never do—improvising a jazz solo, solving a Rubik's cube, barreling down a half-pipe, hanging ten, drafting enchanting essays, landing a quad jump, delivering riveting stand-up, crafting a gourmet meal with leftovers, slamming a 150-mph serve, or pruning shrubs into a topiary zoo—but somewhere along the way, these masters typically, if not almost always, have forfeited what we all still have: the capacity to do a thing simply to do it, for its own sake, even if we do it badly. Play is its own justification.

The attitude of doing a thing simply for its own sake relates directly to one other familiar but critical human activity that must be understood as play or risk being subverted and demeaned into a mere instrumental role leveraged toward some dreadful utilitarian, sensible, and pragmatic outcome. By now it should be clear that worship is far too precious and important an activity to let it degenerate into anything less than play. Our worship of God is far too holy and prized to entrust its form and practice to experts and professionals who, we are told, know what they are doing. Worship is precisely one of those things that if worth doing is worth doing badly. Not every voice is resonant and confident in recitation, but we all confess the creed. Very few voices are worthy of anyone's attention, much less worth recording, but we all must open our mouths and sing our praise to God. Not every preacher can craft a sermon that is impeccably researched, brilliantly developed, and then eloquently delivered. Not every musician guiding the congregation is among the greatest to have ever taken a seat on the keyboard bench. Worship is the task of us all, and that means that it is a task that will be accomplished by mere amateurs and hacks and failed stars. It will be done by those who by rights should have no business doing it but who do it anyway because they must. And we all must because we all are human. But since every one of us must be engaged in the pursuit, we can be very sure that the pursuit will often be done badly—at least in the eyes of and according to the standards of the world. But mercifully and consistently, God does not see what man sees or hear what man hears or judge by what man perceives. What humans do badly he welcomes and receives as beautiful.

It bears reiterating that acknowledging the inherent mediocrity that will define not only our worship but also our lives is never an excuse for apathetic efforts, lame attempts, or contentment with the inferior and unexceptional. Humans living in sync with God's plan will strive to advance upward and forward in every endeavor, from pickleball to singing alto in a chorale, or from lawncare to parenting. Complacency and satisfaction with human inability and failure is not the way of those who follow Christ. But while we strive and expend real effort at the things we have been given to do, we are realistic, and far more importantly, we are aimed not at achievement and triumph but at simply being a participant in the beautiful things we do. We delight that we are able to play. Never is this truer than in our worship of God, whether as individuals or as congregations. This is the argument made in the very title of Marva Dawn's book about Christian living and faithful worship, *A Royal Waste of Time.*[9] She is right. Worship does not have to justify the expenditure of time or resources. It is its own justification. Worship is play. Liturgy is play. It is done for the sheer delight of doing it. It is done for its own sake and never with an ulterior or pragmatic end lying behind or beneath as justification. Preaching and listening and reciting and reading and liturgy and singing are all aspects of worship that happen outside of ordinary time and in the context of play, which is time that inherently points us to the eternal. And when done in Christ, worship wholeheartedly celebrates the eternal truths and promises of God. Christians worship because they must. As human, they can do nothing less. And we dare not entrust our worship to experts or professionals or superstars. There is always a better preacher, organist, praise band, or liturgist somewhere else, and a person can easily squander a lifetime of Sundays searching the world or the internet for the best. But worship defies such corrupt and wicked thinking. Worship is play. It is the province of the amateur. It is the task of everyman. It is worth doing badly.

The old adage chides us for worshiping our work, working at our play, and playing at worship. While the first two certainly

9 Marva J. Dawn, *A Royal Waste of Time: The Splendor of Worshiping God and Being the Church for the World* (Grand Rapids: Eerdmans, 1999).

are failures of our humanity, the third, it turns out, is actually the exact right way to operate. If only we would all be better at playing at our worship instead of elevating, commodifying, professionalizing, perfecting, and destroying it. Christians need to learn to love play. We need to embrace the purposelessness and wastefulness of play. We need to play for the sake of play. Learning to play is a necessary life skill that humans too often try hard to lose. Christians should push back against the denigration of play. Part of Christian witness to the world is showing the world how to play in our worship, in our marriages, in our homes, in our friendships, in our neighborhoods, and yes, even in our workplaces. Play is God's good gift to people. And so, of course, is the remaining topic of our chapter: sleep.

THE ABSURDITY OF SLEEP

It would not be hard to make a convincing case that the most astounding and awe-inspiring things humans encounter are the mundane realities that happen around us and to us with such routine predictability that we hardly notice them, let alone accord them their deserved status as breathtaking marvels. Luther liked to call attention to these ordinary and usually overlooked aspects of life that defied human explanation or understanding and deserved to be recognized with reverent awe. A caterpillar "dead" in a cocoon only to emerge in splendor; a towering oak grown from a stone-like acorn; the ability to communicate news, ideas, and truth through human speech and writing, the daily rising of the sun; the miracle of music: all of these should provoke those who are observant to stunned wonder and to the praise of the God who made it all so. I'm convinced that one of those routinely overlooked mundane wonders that deserves a bit more of our attention is sleep.

Interestingly, those in the fields of the hard sciences, as well as those still granted use of the science label but in softer forms, have shown in recent years increasing interest in better understanding sleep, yet still they seem to have barely scratched the surface. While there is a wealth of research underway to better discern the processes, purposes, and impacts of sleep, there remain vast reaches of uncharted territory and even fundamental questions yet to be studied and explained. It appears that sleep is not as simple as we may assume. Aware of my glaring scholarly limitations, I won't venture any thoughts on the extraordinarily complicated physiological properties of sleep, and I'll let the psychological and even philosophical aspects of sleep be the preoccupation of graduate students with the requisite level of interest and funding. For my purposes, those perspectives on sleep can be left to the side. I am content to take up an angle that garners precious little attention in the academy or even the church: the theological aspects of sleep. Not even theologians are inclined to pay much attention to something so utterly ordinary and earthbound as sleep.

One does not necessarily need to think like a theologian, however, to arrive at what seems a rather obvious observation. Try to step back and think about it from a distance, and perhaps you'll agree with me, or perhaps not; but the more I think about it, the more it seems to me that it is just plain weird that humans sleep. We are sentient, rational beings who pride ourselves on our independence and autonomy and our ability to control situations and master circumstances. We like to be the kings and queens of our own lives: lords of our living and authors of our reality. Yet, every sixteen hours or so, unless something infringes on our routine, we surrender our rationality, abdicate the throne, relinquish all control, and renounce adulthood to regress back into infancy as we unconditionally surrender to our need for sleep. How strange that *Homo sapiens* sleeps—and a great deal at that. The average full-functioning adult, at the peak of human development, still devotes a third of his precious, limited hours of life every single day to the out-of-life, virtual nonexistence that is sleep. And yet, besides the obvious fact that our bodies demand it, there is no compelling reason why we should be creatures that sleep.

One of the most remarkable aspects of the present quest to understand sleep is that the most basic question about sleep still has no answer: Why do humans, along with practically every other member of the entire animal kingdom, need to sleep? We all do it. It's a given. When Joe Raposo sang his catchy, but surreptitiously soothing, tune "Everybody Sleeps" on *Sesame Street*, no one saw the need to protest, and there was no shortage of humorous video to make the two minutes of melody visually entertaining. Sleep is just part of life, and everyone does it. Yet the astounding truth is that no one knows for sure just why it is that everybody sleeps. It is not merely to rest our bodies. That task can be accomplished without the need for sleep. Appropriate periods of inaction are sufficient to allow muscles and body parts to repair and reenergize for another bout of human busy-ness. One thing that does seem clear is that it is not our bodies that need sleep but our brains; but what is not at all clear is why exactly our brains need to sleep. Considered from the standpoint of evolutionary theory, one can only wonder why man has not managed to evolve his way out of his need for sleep. Certainly other animals—even ones we are told deserve our respect for the complexity of their social structures and intelligence, like dolphins—manage to function with sleep of such an altered nature and with so little of it that it is hardly recognizable as sleep. And when we humans undertake to design and build machines to accomplish important tasks for us, we do not engineer into the plan a need for an extended time of sleep every few hours. Factory assembly lines, 787s, and mobile phones don't need to sleep in order to function; they just need fuel and working parts. Machines are not rejuvenated for work through something called sleep—even when my Mac pretends to sleep, it's actually just conserving energy. If machines we build and even other animals are able to get by without it, why are humans still so dependent on such an intrusive degradation of our human achievement and stature as sleep?

From an evolutionary or purely biological standpoint, the extreme degree of man's dependence on sleep does not make much sense; if it weren't so ubiquitously normal for every single one of us every single day of our lives—a reality forced and inflicted on every one of us before we can make it through even a single 24-hour cycle—we'd be incredulous that the most advanced creature in the world nevertheless remains hopelessly reliant on something so unsophisticated, primitive, and humbling as sleep. Sleepers are insensible. They are vulnerable. They are easy prey for predators and all manner of evil. Sleepers are unthinking, passive, unproductive, incapable, and helpless as infants in their dependence. Sleepers emerge from bed in serious need of sprucing up. That humans sleep is inexplicable from the standpoint of all the traits that humans value: engagement, activity, pleasure, attractiveness, efficiency, dominance, control, autonomy, and pride. Considered objectively and scientifically, sleep makes no sense. It is absurd. But considered spiritually and theologically, sleep is a brilliantly beautiful thing.

Whatever scientific solution eventually achieves consensus status as the right answer to the question about the human need for sleep, a far more compelling theological explanation is already at hand. Theology can handle the perplexing problem of why we sleep with an answer that is as compelling and potent as it is simple and elegant. If we believe that God is the creator and that God—and not the impersonal machinations of evolutionary law—produced man as he now is, then the obvious reason for man's uncanny utter dependence on daily sleep is that God made man this way. From the beginning, sleep was part of the plan. It was God's idea that man should sleep away a full third of his life. God designed man to wake each morning as one reborn into existence and then to arrive at the end of a day of working, playing, contemplating, and delighting in God and creation depleted physically, mentally, emotionally, and perhaps even spiritually and in desperate need of sleep. God made man to need to sleep every single day. There is nothing anywhere in the scriptural record to indicate that sleep itself is an anomaly or an aspect of the curse after the fall. In fact, quite the opposite is true, and sound sleep is seen as a gift from God to his faithful creatures. So, why did God make us this way, as creatures who need an extended period of time each day when we return to the posture and status of babies? Why do we need to sleep? The simple theological answer is that sleep is the daily declaration that humans live only and always as God's contingent creatures. It can never and will never be otherwise.

Sleep is an undeniable, intrusive, daily decree written into our brains and bodies that humans are nothing but creatures who are dependent, fragile, and in desperate need of something they cannot choose or achieve. Sleep does not comply to our demands or conform to our plans. As anyone knows who has tried, it does not work to decide to fall asleep. We have all been in the unpleasant situation of plotting a strategic violation of our sacred hours of sleep: an early alarm to catch an early flight, to get a predawn start on a hike, or to prepare the house for early guests; or perhaps our going to bed was somehow drastically delayed, and now we are desperate to fall asleep as soon as possible to maximize what little sleeping time is left. Of course, as we each know from hard experience, the very determination to fall quickly and deeply asleep dooms the entire process. It will not happen. The effort to will oneself to sound sleep all but guarantees that sleep will not come—unless God mercifully intervenes and grants sleep to his wretchedly helpless creature.

FAITH IN THE GIFT

Even unbelievers and pagans recognize that sleep is not ours to choose. The sandman must make his rounds, or Hypnos or Somnus are sought to bestow the blessing of sleep to the weary human hungry for what he cannot will or grasp for himself. The very thing we need to survive, the thing without which we will certainly die, must be given to us apart from our own effort or decision. Sleep compels us to admit the truth of our fundamental neediness and dependence. Sleep forces us to face our own creaturely humanity. We are not lords. We are not in charge. We are not autonomous. We are not in control. The truth of our utter dependence on God, a truth insulting and confounding to those determined to be their own masters and the lords of their own lives, is for Christians sheer joy and utter delight. From the standpoint of faith, there is nothing better than to be the creature of God. In an engaging essay reflecting on the wonder of sleep, Marc Barnes offers a definition of sleep as theologically rich as it is eloquent: "To be asleep is to enjoy being in the mode of a creature which receives its being from another; it is to be helpless; given over; one who does not have oneself deliberately at hand."[10] What a great line that is: "does not have one-

10 Marc Barnes, "Insomnia and Idolatry," *New Polity Magazine*, no. 1.3 (2020): 62.

self deliberately at hand." Indeed—to sleep is to lose ready access not only to the world around but even to oneself. People who sleep cannot control their own thoughts or even bodies as dreams and sleep paralysis respectively prove. To sleep is to be altogether out of control, which means, of course, that sleep is a particularly Christian practice. After all, "out of control" is the definitive posture for all who would rightly consider or conduct the Christian way of life.

Christians live all their lives out of control. It is true of the beginning, middle, and end of life. What is more out of control than an infant dangling over a font or a body one final breath from being a corpse? That Christians in between sometimes think themselves in control is the delusion of sin. To live life out of control is the essence of faith. God is God, and we are not. God gives, and we receive. God calls the shots, and we follow as directed. Sleep is the overwhelmingly powerful daily reality that imposes itself on every single human to verify and reinforce the fact of every human's desperately needy creatureliness. Sleep fits perfectly into a Christian confession of reality. Since God created it, how could it not? At bottom, sleep is all about faith. The person who lies down to sleep must harbor some degree of confidence that he will wake again. Without that hope, sleep is an overwhelming terror. But how can a person be sure of anything when she is helpless, vulnerable, and insensible? Sleep demands faith—or barring that, a reliable lookout or solid doors and sturdy locks. Daniel Everett titled the engrossing account of his life in the Amazonian jungle creating a written language for the Pirahã tribe (a story finally tragic as it becomes the memoir of his loss of faith in Christ) *Don't Sleep, There Are Snakes*.[11] This pithy advice, he reveals, was the minimally animistic tribe's

11 Daniel L. Everett, *Don't Sleep, There Are Snakes: Life and Language in the Amazonian Jungle* (New York: Vintage Departures, 2008).

standard version of "good night." It seems fair to see more than mere cultural differences at work here. If there is no God who creates, redeems, provides, and restores, then who is going to look out for you when you are asleep? When you're on your own, it's best that you don't sleep. Bad things happen when you sleep. Sleep is inherently risky; but for those who live in faith, risk is transformed into trust.

It is no surprise, then, that sleep is so often a challenge for so many people today, even for those living far from snake-infested jungles and with at least one deadbolt on every exterior door. Any cultural reality that seeks to function without God will inevitably struggle to come to terms with sleep. Without a God, or at least someone moderately trustworthy, keeping watch over life, how can anyone trust themselves to sleep? Sleep becomes an overwhelming and impossible burden: one must have it, but one cannot afford to risk it. Desperate to find some manageable solution to the problem of sleep, Americans spent over $2 billion exclusively on sleep-aid drugs in 2020. Add to that all of the other efforts contrived to make sleep possible and the sleep market is estimated at over $40 billion each year. And yet the problems persist: insomnia, somniphobia, night terrors, daytime tiredness, and more. While there are certainly physical issues that lack any direct spiritual overtones which may interfere with sleep, the required faith aspect of peaceful sleep holds as a general truth even when it does not specifically apply to a given situation. Struggles with sleep simply manifest our deeper struggles to make sense of life and to manage the challenges of life relying only on ourselves. It is absolutely an issue of faith. People who can't trust can't sleep. And if you are unfortunate enough to put your trust in the wrong place, you could end up staked to the ground with a tent peg driven through your temple—or worse. There are plenty of people who, like Sisera, sleep peacefully but foolishly, thoroughly enchanted by their fraudulent protector yet utterly deluded by their misplaced trust in themselves, other creatures, or demonic false gods of the invisible realm. Secure and peaceful sleep comes only to those who live in faith in the God who has made himself known in the life, death, and resurrection of Jesus Christ.

THE BIBLICAL STORY

While the Bible issues some pointed warnings about the folly of wrongly trusting those who watch while we sleep, from the whittled tip of Jael's tent peg to the honed razor of Delilah's Philistine barber, there is also an abundance of references in the Bible to the afflictions that steal peaceful sleep from those who, for whatever reason, are not in a right relationship with God. Anxious pharaohs and distraught pagan kings are denied sleep, wandering and fleeing patriarchs and prophets have their sleep interrupted by divine messages that demand full attention, bodily weary and emotionally spent disciples also testify to their helplessness before the power of sleep as they fall victim to its stern demands in spite of appeals and warnings straight from the mouth of God—meanwhile, the Messiah himself living in full faith and trust sleeps in perfect peace in a boat's stern while wind and waves shriek all around. Sleep is a key plot element in God's story, which unfolds in the pages of the Bible. Recognizing the strangely mysterious but undeniably imperious role that sleep plays in every human life, it makes sense that sleep would be granted so central a role at vital junctures in the narrative. The tragedy of the human condition—with its outward pretense of self-assured strength and steady control over every situation that merely, and poorly, masks a raging internal turmoil, angst, and fragility—is captured perfectly by man's worldly bravado that collapses each evening into a servile and fawning posture toward his indifferent and often cruel master, sleep, who is deaf to entreaties and delights to demean his subjects by consistently reducing them to the status of helpless babies. The biblical record fully grasps how very odd and how very humbling it is that we humans must sleep every day.

The Bible also knows that peaceful and restful sleep is always and only an act of divine grace that must be received solely as gift or forfeited. Sleep is never claimed as a right and is never submissive to an act of human will. So David, encouraging a mindset aimed at reflective contemplation later named leisure, acknowledges God's sovereign role in providing the security necessary for sleep. The psalmist counsels his readers, both ancient and modern, to live in the confident trust of faith that makes bedtime peace possible:

> Tremble, and do not sin;
>   Meditate in your heart upon your bed, and be still. . . .
> In peace I will both lie down and sleep,
>   For You alone, O Lord, make me to dwell in safety.[12]

Later, David's son and royal successor, Solomon, relates some of his own divinely granted, but personally and painfully corroborated, wisdom—wisdom that encapsulates many of the themes of this book but especially the union of grace and faith at the core of sleep:

---

12 Psalm 4:4, 8.

Unless the Lord watches over the city,
the watchman stays awake in vain.
It is in vain that you rise up early and go late to rest,
eating the bread of anxious toil;
for He gives to His beloved sleep.[13]

God alone is the giver of sleep, and he gives this singularly enriching gift to his beloved, to his chosen. So, Jesus, God's chosen Messiah, sleeps in peace and invites those he chooses to live in faith, trust his promise, and sleep in peace.

Jesus, who sleeps and who admonishes his disciples for their inability to control their own poorly timed sleep in Gethsemane—another bitter reminder that sleep is the master, and humans the supplicant subjects—clearly operates with an understanding of the direct correlation and interrelation between faith and sleep and death. The connection lies near at hand throughout the Bible and in human experience, but Jesus sharpens and cements it. Jesus declares that the little girl is only asleep and later tells his obtuse and literalist disciples the same about Lazarus.[14] The point is not only that for Jesus calling a corpse back from death is as routine and incidental as waking a child for school or a friend for breakfast, though it is that. Neither is the correspondence between sleep and death merely the apparent tangible parallels: horizontal and stretched out or curled into a fetal ball, unmoving, eyes closed, insensible,

13 Psalm 127:1b–2 (ESV).
14 See Mark 5:39; John 11:11.

checked-out of life.[15] No, for Jesus, for the Creator and Lord of this world and its people, sleep and death run together in the context of faith. They should be understood as on a continuum. Sleep is a daily ending of living, a forced break from the routine of life. Sleep compels the confession of human contingency and pounds home the truth that we are not in control. Without faith that someone is keeping watch and that one will wake again, sleep is an impossible burden, a source of angst and terror. All of these truths hold with regard also to death, but there they are pushed to their extreme.

There is benefit in considering a bit more fully the tight bond between sleep and death that runs through the biblical narrative and that is basic to our Christian confession. The enduring strength of the connection is evident each time we reference the death of a Christian brother or sister as "falling asleep in Jesus." Still, beyond even all the manifest congruity between sleep and death already noted, the best connection is one not so often encountered or exploited. In our daily human endeavors, it's not uncommon to experience a yearning for the day's end; especially at the end of a hard day, we look forward to lying down to sleep. People will even describe the moment

15 The obvious parallels between sleep and death, as well as the latent lessons available when one sees preparing for sleep as preparation for death, were beautifully captured by Paul Gerhardt's exceptionally potent and poignant verse of "Now Rest Beneath Night's Shadow," a verse that sadly failed to survive into synodically approved hymnals beyond *The Lutheran Hymnal* (554:4):

To rest my body hasteth,
Aside its garments casteth,
    Types of mortality;
These I put off and ponder
How Christ will give me yonder
    A robe of glorious majesty.

of head hitting pillow as the best part of the day. But, unless we are abusing sleep as an escape hatch out of painful and unresolvable realities that confront us in present life, we know that we never welcome sleep as the goal but as merely a means toward the goal. I don't yearn for sleep because I can't wait to spend 6.75 hours insensible, paralyzed, vulnerable, and entertained or tormented by a nonsensical stream of mismatched brain files jammed together in a bewildering mash-up of surreal quasi-existence. Sleep is the blissful reward at the end of the day because it is good to be able to quit and yield to God. Yet, sweet as it may be, sleep is not the objective—waking from sleep is the objective. And even the greatest champions of sleep will have to admit that only those who have been overrun by the oppression of sin and have despaired of life altogether would ever consider the shadowy existence of sleep to be superior to life in the world of the awake. Sleep is just the passage to something else much better.

For the Christian, death is the same. Death is not ever the goal. We never aim at death. The goal is what lies on the other side. The goal is waking from death. The goal is the resurrection of the dead on the Last Day. In his great mercy and extravagant grace, God not only gives his people hope for the future, but he floods our lives now with blessings, goodness, joy, beauty, delights, and truth that defy description. Yet as good as those things are, falling asleep in Jesus is better—better by far, which is saying a lot. Christians anticipate death not with terror or dread but in much that same way that they look forward to rolling into bed, disappearing beneath the heavy covers, and falling into a deep sleep at the end of a very long, cold day. And yet, tantalizing as that picture may be, resting securely and blissfully in the presence of Jesus after death, freed from the reach of sin and delighting in God's perfect grace, is not yet the end. Even that joy will be superseded by a still greater reality: the day when Jesus stands at the edge of your grave and, like a parent standing near your bed, calls you by name and gently insists that it is time for you to shake off your sleep, get up out of the grave, and greet the new day. He'll give you a hand up into the new heavens and new earth of his eternal kingdom, and then you can get busy living as the creature he always planned for you to be. Death, like sleep, is merely the means toward more living. Sleep and death are but interludes in the fullness of living in God's great reality.

RECEIVING THE LIMIT

Sleep, then, is God's daily gift not only for the sake of our brains but for the sake of our self-understanding, for the sake of our faith relationship with God, for the sake of our living well in this world as the creatures that we are, and for the sake of our eternal hope. And in the context of this book's interest in work, leisure, and sabbath, sleep helps us see once again how the fundamental realities and givens of our human being and existence mesh seamlessly with the theological argument I've sought to build that life is most rightly and helpfully understood as *vita receptiva*. Sleep is an essential and conspicuous part of the circadian rhythm that orients and norms a fully formed human life. We live our lives well when we live them in harmony with what God has established as true for humans—when we live them in sync with what is. This means that life works when we are receiving and welcoming what God gives.

This is profoundly true of sleep. To fight against our built-in need for sleep is folly. Those who refuse to yield enough time for sleep diminish life in the present and shave years off its length.

Wisdom teaches us to yield to God's reality and receive what he gives—including the gift of sleep. To reject what God gives and to resist his invitation to live in tune with his plan—in other words, to fail to live in submission to his authority—is the sin of acedia. It is the refusal to receive what the Creator gives and the consequent inability to delight in what the Creator gives. Acedia flattens life and makes it a miserable drudgery devoid of purpose and joy. Sleep reminds us to yield our whole selves and to receive all that God gives.

Sleep also reminds us that we are altogether human. It may seem self-evident, but it is far too easy to forget: God is God, and you are not. We are creatures; we are not God. We must sleep, or we die. God does not sleep, ever. Sleep serves, then, as a stark component of our profound creatureliness. Sleep marks our inherent human limit. Rather than lamenting our limitations as creatures and protesting against the restrictions imposed on us by the Creator, the better course is to rejoice in the fact that we are not saddled with the task of being God or even made to bear the weight of being the lords of our own lives. As humans we have the decided blessing of being mere creatures bound by the requirement to sleep. We have the privilege of being able to drop out of life for a third of each day. But God does not sleep. He is always fully present. That God does not sleep marks his divinity. Idols can't match the divine standard of vigilance or availability. Elijah used the taunt against Team Baal during the Mount Carmel contest to see whose deity could swallow a sacrifice.[16] Even 450 prophets of the false god could not win their absent god's attention. Indifferent to their prayers, their god, Elijah helpfully suggested, must be away on a trip, or awkwardly indisposed in the bathroom, or even asleep and needing

16 See 1 Kings 18:27.

someone to wake him. To be asleep is to be humbled. It is to be out of commission, unavailable, incapable. Such is the hard truth for all creatures, including every idol. But God does not sleep. God is always fully God.

It is good that we do not have to shoulder the burden of being God. It is good to be a creature who sleeps. It is good to be humbled and brought back to our infantile dependence. It is good to end every day by lying down and waiting for God to send sleep, by letting him heal our weariness, refresh our brains, protect us from evil, and run the world without us. Like the farmer who sleeps while God works the miracles of growth and grain, every day we capitulate—we step out of the way, close our eyes, and sleep while God fulfills his promise and brings his plans for our lives to fruition. Like work well done, and leisure centered on God's reality, and sabbath delighting in God's rest, when it is grounded in faith and confessing confident trust, sleep is also an act of worship.

There is certainly much more to our lives than sleep and play, and even this chapter's necessarily cursory look at each of these aspects of life can serve as little more than introduction. And yet, I am convinced that taking time to consider just a bit more thoughtfully both play and sleep, and then learning to see each of them in the bright light of the normative perspective of our Christian faith, will better equip us to approach all the other parts of our life in ways that honor God more fully and serve our neighbor more faithfully. Embracing God's good gifts of play and sleep doubtless will enrich our lives, but far more importantly, doing so will intensify the brilliance of our witness to the world of the great truth and delightful goodness of God's plan for his human creatures. Play and sleep are alike in that both lie outside ordinary time. They are both times within our lives that operate with their own calculation of time. In that way, both sleep and play serve to bracket, circumscribe, and relativize the scope and reach of our daily realities and help to center us in God's greater truth, which reorders and recalibrates all the pressing matters of this present life. In both our play and our sleep, we joyfully confess that we live our lives out of control. Sleep and play matter, then, because both help us learn again to yield our lives and our very selves to the wishes and the agenda of another. And this, of course, lands us once again directly into the middle of Luther's account of the Christian who lives outside of himself—in faith toward God and in love toward neighbor. Whatever we may be doing, there is no better place for any of us to be.

CHAPTER 7

CONCLUSION: LIVING THE RECEPTIVE LIFE

ROOM FOR REENCHANTMENT

Over the last few decades, there have been sporadic but persistent calls from oddly disparate corners of the culture for what has frequently and increasingly been identified as the need for a reenchantment of the world. Such an amorphous neologism allows for a great deal of diversity among those who recognize a problem and yearn for a solution—but agree on neither. Jaundiced by the superficiality of life, jaded by the isolation and loneliness of modern Western existence, disheartened by the threats of technology and humanity's slavery to their devices, distraught over the depletion of the Western soul in the face of an unrelenting radical materialism for which the only real thing is the thing that can be empirically measured, or just nostalgic for simpler more earthbound ways of living, many people are eager for something spiritual or mystical or magical or at least meaningful to augment lives that by their own admission are increasingly vacuous, vapid, and sterile. And most people are savvy enough to recognize that this personal and cultural crisis of disenchantment of the world is not going to be restrained, much less repulsed, with the sort of thinking that assumes all can be made right with a few tweaks of our brave new Enlightenment world, exemplified by the patronizing effort to augment STEM education with an "A" for arts and then applaud itself for the great sensitivity and prowess exhibited in restoring balance and making the world right again with STEAM. Most of those advocating a reenchantment of the world are contending for much more than an art appreciation course taught at the local high school every Tuesday and Friday right after lunch. And the spontaneously expanding gnome village in a shady grove along the edge of the affluent neighborhood park isn't fooling anyone—not even my preschool-age grandchildren.

A strong case can be made that Christians should concur with the lament over the disenchantment of the world and join in the plea for a renewed valuation of things that count beyond the merely pragmatic and provable. Christians do not disavow metaphysical realities, after all. We confess that there is much more to the world than the things we can empirically verify. We should be wary, however, of thinking that every call for a reenchantment of the world is one that faithful followers of Christ should support or, on the other hand, of thinking that anything less than a full-throated, orthodox, Book of Concord version of enchantment is one that we must categorically reject. There is a great deal that lies between misty Druid rituals and belief in angels.

It seems safe to conclude that any call for reenchantment that has its roots in human sentiment or pagan rituals (the difference is ultimately minimal) can be set aside without further ado. Both center attention on the subjective experiences and the perceived personal benefits of whatever spiritual or metaphysical encounter is sought or claimed or valued. Despite the standard and ubiquitous counsel to the contrary, a person does not arrive at spiritual truth or metaphysical meaning by following her heart. What is real must come from outside the self and not from the depths of our corrupt human being, no matter how sincere or heartfelt our thoughts and feelings. What is ultimately real and so a source of genuine enchantment worthy of our awe and determined pursuit is not what we feel or ascertain or conclude; what is real is what God the Creator puts there. God determines reality, and so God himself establishes and implants the foundation of the world that serves then as the only legitimate source capable of producing enchanted wonder and delight among tuned-in creatures who become aware, by God's sustaining mercy and electing grace, of the reality that is outside of themselves, or put more personally and confessionally, reality that is *extra nos*—outside of us. Enchantment can be regained in our flat and mechanistic world, then, only by grounding it in what God actually put there and not in what we feel is there, wish was there, or assert to be there. Those who confess the Creator's lordship of the world should be eager to embrace the marvels of that world, including the great metaphysical facts God himself built into it.

All of this is to say that Bible-believing, confessional, orthodox, and faithful followers of Jesus could do with a little more appreciation of the necessarily enchanted reality of our world. No doubt, Christians like us already make significant metaphysical claims: God exists; angels are real; God joined himself to human flesh; He died, rose again, lives now as Lord of all, and is coming as judge of all; sacraments deliver real grace and eternal blessings; Christians live even after death and on the Last Day will be bodily resurrected like Jesus; and all of creation is going to be re-created as God intended and then continue perfectly for eternity. The Book of Concord is more enchanted than most of us probably realize. It provides a wealth of metaphysical truth that can certainly enchant and enrich our world. And yet, the Christian account of God's world includes still more powerful metaphysical elements that are woven through its fabric beyond even these definitive and essential assertions of God's truth. To rule out of bounds any sort of metaphysical truth beyond what is specifically spelled out in biblical revelation and Christian confession is contemptuous of the fullness of God's creative capacity. God is superabundant in the grace he extends, and that includes instilling in his creation a wealth of profound metaphysical realities that suffuse it, shape it, direct it, and enrich it. Paying attention to these "even more" realities that exist alongside the fixed points of specific Christian doctrine opens the door for Christian people to live typical and routine human lives that are far from ordinary—that are, in fact, delightfully and daily enchanted—that is, filled with wonder, awe, meaning, and inspiration just as God planned for his human creatures.

The metaphysical realities that exist beyond the familiar ones of our confession—foundational realities that bind and guide this world's operations and that were put there by God and which I am convinced especially deserve more considered attention from faithful Christian people—are the three great transcendental realities: truth, goodness, and beauty. I introduced these briefly in chapter 4 in the process of presenting the idea that aesthetics is the face of leisure, but I believe a little more attention to these transcendentals is warranted—especially in the context of thinking about living the fullness of the receptive life. For millennia, these central realities of existence in this world have been recognized and appreciated by careful thinkers and artists in every field of inquiry. That the three transcendentals have recently fallen into virtual obscurity, even among those deemed educated, certainly validates the acute need to reenchant our world. As admitted before, the presentation of a full case defending and unpacking the classic, threefold, metaphysical foundation of the created world—truth, goodness, and beauty—lies well beyond the scope of this book.[1] But

1 To become better acquainted with the transcendentals and why they matter, one can begin with C. S. Lewis's *The Abolition of Man* (New York: Harper One, 1944, 2001); and then if necessary, read a more contemporary presentation from Stephen R. Turley, *Awakening Wonder: A Classical Guide to Truth, Goodness & Beauty* (Camp Hill, PA: Classical Academic Press, 2014) or Jordan Cooper, *In Defense of the True, the Good, and the Beautiful: On the Loss of Transcendence and the Decline of the West* (Ithaca, NY: Just and Sinner Publications, 2021).

spending a bit more time considering each of these realities and offering some reflection on their place within God's created world will perhaps serve as impetus for faithful followers of Christ to work more resolutely and deliberately toward the reenchantment of our world, or at least the immediate world of their own lives. Additionally, coming to terms with the three transcendentals and their significance will prove quite relevant and useful for the overall purpose of this chapter and entire book: thinking faithfully about our lives in light of sabbath.

THE THREE TRANSCENDENTALS

Affirming and appreciating the three transcendental realities, realities that can't be unequivocally and empirically verified or proved but that simply exist by virtue of God's will, does not equate with being mystical. Lest the reader have any doubts about my motives, I am not one who suffers from even the slightest inclination toward anything remotely mystical nor am I one to be driven by emotions. But what God has designed into his world matters, and what he has built into every part of his world is the intermeshed realities of truth, goodness, and beauty. Each of these great realities exists independent of any cause or source other than God. Each one defines itself. That we know the importance of each and also grasp the functional definition of each—even if we cannot begin to articulate such a definition—substantiates the foundational and all-encompassing nature of truth, goodness, and beauty. These are things that matter fundamentally for their own sakes. They are the bedrock and the guiding parameters of our lives.

What is true is what coheres with what God has deemed to be. Truth is not empirically or scientifically verified, nor is it determined by what "feels right." Truth is what aligns with what God has established. It is true that God created all that exists.

It is true that Jesus died and rose from the dead. It is true that God gives his grace to humans through the means of sacraments. It is true that a watermelon dropped from a rooftop will fall . . . and fast. Truth simply means that a thing is so because God has made it so. The next transcendental, the good, is likewise grounded in the work of the Creator. What is good is what is in step with God's will. What is good is not determined by precedent, majority rule, utility, or human conscience. Situations do not determine what is good, nor do people. It is good that a man and woman marry and have children. It is good that we die to ourselves and live for the other. It is good that we delight in obeying the Commandments. God determines what is good. Beauty, the third and often forgotten transcendental, naturally, operates in the same way. What is beautiful is what manifests and expresses God's glory; it points to him and his reality. Beauty is certainly not in the eye of the beholder. Beauty is not a matter of taste or culture. Beauty is not what creates certain feelings or responses in us. Beauty is what honors God and furthers his purpose for the world. It is beautiful when the physical world is operating as God intended—and every day confronts us with overwhelming natural beauty all around us. It is beautiful when humans freely serve those around them. It is beautiful when God's love is displayed; and so it is that Christ crucified is profoundly beautiful. God defines beauty even as he defines truth and goodness.

Truth, goodness, and beauty are built deep into the structures and operations of the entire creation, including human creatures. Each of the transcendentals corresponds to a particular aspect of our human being. Truth correlates closely with mind and rationality. Truth is focused on the *logos*, that is, the word or principle that undergirds and directs all of our thinking and knowing. Truth is the domain of doctrine, which is nothing more than a record of God's doings and so God's truth. Goodness is present in our human actions. It maps to the ancient Greek idea of *ethos*, or way of being and doing. Goodness is the center of the study of ethics, which is nothing more than an exploration and presentation of what man should be and do. Finally, beauty is most strongly connected to human emotions or feelings or passions. The Greeks called this domain *pathos*. Of course, to express beauty as related to feelings already sadly diminishes our understanding of the importance of beauty, as our contemporary world persists in weighting feelings or emotions much lower than thinking and rationality. As heirs of the Enlightenment West, it is an enduring part of our inheritance to privilege intellect to the point of excluding any role for feeling. Pushing back against this marginalizing of *pathos* as opposed to *logos* and even *ethos* is one of the objectives of this chapter.[2] Beauty, to complete the triptych of the transcendentals, is the object of aesthetics.

The point of thinking about each of the transcendentals in relation to the human person is not to rank them or choose a favorite. The point is to see that these three transcendentals are at the core of the human being in her complete personhood: mind, actions, and emotions are each thoroughly engaged and wholly taken into account when we encounter the transcendentals and so the entire human is exhaustively considered according to the fullness of what makes her human. What else is a person beyond her thinking, her acting, and her feeling? *Logos*, *ethos*, and *pathos* capture the essence of what makes man, man. And truth, goodness, and beauty give to man the criteria

2 For those who are interested, I argued for the importance of reappropriating the critical place of *ethos* in my book *A Case for Character: Towards a Lutheran Virtue Ethics* (Minneapolis: Fortress, 2014).

by which to operate well in life, as well as provide the target for the fullest expression of his humanity as he strives to live fully in truth, goodness, and beauty. God's beauty trains human *pathos* to feel as humans should—grieving what is false and evil and thus ugly and delighting in what is true and good and thus beautiful.

Our Western world has operated with a hierarchy that privileges mind and rationality over all else for many long centuries. The roots of this go far back in our history, but they were brought to their pinnacle with the Enlightenment emphasis on the primacy of rational human thought in every human pursuit, including the understanding and place of truth, goodness, and beauty. The Enlightenment put man at the center of the world, and man put mind at the center of man. The results of this hierarchy are familiar to us all. We operate with this as our default, taken-for-granted way of thinking, choosing, planning, and living. And while our culture certainly concedes significance to individual feelings, dispassionate intellect with its highest cultural expression in what is deferentially credentialed as hard science is still universally acknowledged as the final authority. The church is not immune to this supremacy of mind. Though it varies by ecclesiastical tradition, doctrine or "Bible teaching" is typically revered as the most important part of Christian confession, with active doing or ethics in a secondary, supporting role, and then, if pressed to admit or realize its existence, beauty trails along behind as a distant afterthought, an embellishment as time and energy allow once all the weighty doctrinal and ethical issues have been satisfactorily addressed.

This hierarchy, entitling mind and *logos* above all else, is never truer than among the people of my own heritage. As previously noted, Lutherans are prone to adore doctrine, tolerate ethics, and dismiss beauty. It is hard for them to imagine that something so subjective and murky as beauty matters more than a mere frill or accoutrement to be considered for adoption or purchase only when it can be comfortably afforded. The very notion that beauty counts as much as morality, let alone as much as propositional truth, likely strikes most Christians as patently ridiculous. Yet this is precisely the point: truth, goodness, and beauty always operate together as the core both of God's world and of our human being. One cannot embrace and cultivate a love for one without doing the same for the others. Most Christians understand this on a certain level; they acknowledge that holding fastidiously to right teaching while denying God's command in the course of their actions amounts to a false confession. No doubt, it is difficult to argue with this position since James says exactly that, and so does Paul, and so does Jesus.[3] But the connection extends also to beauty. What is superficial, artificial, shoddy, half-baked, deflating, and ugly is not true and is not good. It violates all three transcendentals. Ugliness or just the lack of beauty and the tolerance of kitsch is much more than a failure in taste; it is a failure in what is true and good.

The notion that beauty is nothing but a matter of individual taste or merely a matter of personal preference is one of the colossal lies that have been perpetrated on modern man and sadly found eager acceptance in all corners of our culture, even in the church. It has become a ubiquitously approved, never questioned axiom. But it is wrong. Beauty is not subjective. Beauty resonates with God's reality and delights in what gives praise to God. To ignore the place of beauty in our communities, in our churches, in our homes, and in our lives is to

3 See James 2:14–17; Romans 8:12–17; Luke 10:30–37, respectively.

impoverish our humanity. Beauty is not a luxury for the elite, but it is a necessity for the full human thriving of every human being. Confessional Christians need to be as concerned about cultivating in people right feelings that are in tune with beauty and that delight in beauty for its own sake as they are about teaching people to love the truth and to honor goodness. And in the same way that the love and pursuit of truth and goodness do not demand a significant outlay of financial resources, neither does the love and pursuit of beauty. All three transcendentals thrive in people's lives with the investment of concerted time and energy, neither of which are resources exclusive to the affluent.

It is important to remember that just as humans are a composite of many discernible parts yet a single reality, so it is with the transcendentals. We can identify three, but the divisions between them are not hard and fast and not easily distinguished; and one cannot ignore or diminish the place of one without harming all three. Truth, goodness, and beauty always run together in harmony. They do not contradict, operate at cross-purposes, or exist in a paradox or even a tension. Rather, they always work in unison as distinct aspects of a single unity of God's purpose in the creation. And, it should be noted, one does not necessarily need to derive the transcendentals from God's very being for them to be the normative and authoritative reality for the entire creation. It is enough that God established them for his creation. This is a point worth stressing since it is always wise in the realm of theology and human thinking to maintain with great care an infinite degree of difference between God and his creation—God is God, and we are not. Of course, even that distinction is set on its head when God himself shattered the distance between God and man forever in the incarnation; but that miracle serves to highlight the utter distinction between God and his creation. In the world in which we live, the transcendentals operate, then, as a single reality, which serves as the ultimate foundation and frame of all that is and specifically of our humanity. So, those who would live in tune with the Creator and the creation must learn to live in tune with the great realities of truth, goodness, and beauty.

Finally, it needs to be mentioned, in defense of *pathos*, or feelings, that experiencing feelings across the gamut of human sensations—the training of which should be seen as the ultimate objective of aesthetics—is definitively not at odds with a Christian way of life. Persuaded of the importance of doctrine that is associated with clear thinking, it is not uncommon for Christians to be too easily dismissive not only of beauty but of the emotional aspect of our humanity that helps us discern beauty. But learning to think rightly and to act rightly are not the only skills that must be learned to live rightly. One must also learn to feel rightly. All three transcendentals, including especially beauty, should be adopted as apt targets for intentional efforts toward formation into the Christian life. The warmth that floods and suddenly swallows you whole when surrounded by those you love on the eve of Christmas; unbidden and unchecked tears of happiness as Frodo is reunited with the Fellowship . . . and Sam; an unanticipated frisson that runs from head to toe as the sopranos soar to heaven, "For Christ is coming, is coming soon" at the climax of "E'en So, Lord Jesus, Quickly Come"; the awestruck, silent, sacred elation walking across a lawn made new by lightning-charged rain and colored dusty gold by the setting sun breaking through the clouds—all of these feelings are the essence of beauty. All of them are true. All of them are good. And learning to see and appreciate them as vital aspects of our human being is a profoundly worthy pursuit.

There is much to learn; all around us every day there is so much that is true and good and beautiful and deserving of our attention and gratitude: the flicker of a million aspen leaves caught in the slightest glimmer of the first morning breeze, the sharp rasping as the October wind blows through a vast field of towering cornstalks with heavy ears, the smile of your grandchild, your spouse's hand finding yours, joining your voice with hundreds of others led by a jubilant organ with all the stops pulled and fairly bellowing the final verse of "For All the Saints" until the globus sensation in your throat finally wins and you let those around you carry the song while you mutely watch familiar faces streaming in through gates of pearl. Feelings that point us to beauty, that resonate with what is true and what is good, are the essence of our human existence.

FORWARD TO THE SABBATH

There is, no doubt, so very much more that can be said, and that arguably needs to be said, about the importance of regaining an understanding and appreciation of the transcendentals in the church and so helping to reenchant the ordinary lives of Christian people. But that task must fall to others, and this chapter needs to find its way back to the topic at hand: work, leisure, and the receptive life that binds them and that delights in sabbath rest. The connection between the three transcendental realities and sabbath should be obvious enough. When God created the universe exactly as he planned, this included building into it the truth, the goodness, and the beauty that we creatures are able to perceive and pursue as creatures should. That same creation shot through with the transcending realities of the true, the good, and the beautiful is the one God celebrated on that very first seventh day when the work was complete and the festival declared. Sabbath is the awareness of the goodness of the creation and of the goodness, power, wisdom, and love of the Creator who made it so. Since sabbath keys on the goodness of the creation, it also then, by extension, is a celebration of the truth and the beauty that God has built into the creation itself. When human creatures are living as God intended, they delight in all that he created, and that means they live in a way that is in tune with the truth, goodness, and beauty that are everywhere present in the creation because God made them everywhere present in the creation.

Enthusiastic as I am in promoting the richness and rightness of living in light of all three transcendentals and learning to delight in and to treasure truth, goodness, and beauty, it needs not only to be noted but to be stressed, however, that while God certainly created and established each of these realities according to his plan, they absolutely do not serve as avenues for fallen man to regain a right relationship with God. It is categorically impossible to achieve unity with God through the pursuit of truth or goodness or beauty. Nevertheless, this idea is, clearly enough, the very thing that most people assume as a given and what virtually all religions and all forms of spirituality routinely and emphatically teach. Following either his reason or his actions or his feelings—that is, tracking either the intellectual, the moral, or the mystical pathway of his human being—seems like it should be the best possible way for a man to connect with metaphysical reality. And this is precisely the counsel that the world's religions offer as the means for a person to find spiritual wholeness or enlightenment or union with God, or whatever is named as the objective of human living.

Perversely, even Christianity can be contorted into such an anthropocentric means of salvation, which is sought through sincere human effort, whether through thinking and believing or acting and accomplishing or feeling and expressing. The deeds of deadly works-righteousness, it must be remembered, are not only the good works of faultless and genuine morality but can also be the grand works of surpassing emotional control or breathtakingly pure mystical ascent or even the works of staunchly unwavering doctrinal confession and fidelity. But carefully preserving and sincerely believing perfect doctrine does not save any more than relentlessly doing right things or ecstatically climbing spiritual heights. Faithful Christian confession is unequivocally clear that all human efforts, whether rational, moral, or mystical, are nothing but demonic self-salvation; they deny and trample the grace and redemption fully accomplished in Christ's Calvary work and Easter resurrection celebration. The transcendentals are not the means to human salvation or even human fulfillment. One does not climb to heaven using his wisdom and intellect, his effort and morality, or his feelings and spirituality. One is saved and made fully human only by living rightly related to the creation and to the Creator, and this is accomplished only in and through Jesus Christ. The gospel of grace is the one and only means of salvation, the one and only way to return to God. This is all profoundly and centrally true. Still, it is also true that these timelessly alluring transcendentals were created by God and built into the creation for the benefit and the delight of his human creatures. We also need to remember that embracing truth and goodness and beauty does not inevitably eventuate in trusting them as means for salvation.

Living in the fullness of God's sabbath means two things: being right with God the Creator, a gift and accomplishment of the gospel alone, and being right with the creation, a gift and accomplishment worked in us by God as we learn to live in tune with the realities of God's natural law grounded in truth, goodness, and beauty. The person who lives in the sabbath knows God and his reality—he knows what is true, good, and beautiful. Sabbath and natural law and the transcendentals are all bound up together. To be fully human, to be all that God created a person to be, is simply to know and to celebrate the wonder of God and his created reality. Pieper was getting at precisely this idea when he declared, "Leisure is steeping oneself in the whole of creation."[4] Remember that Pieper's call for leisure, for scholia, is ultimately a call for living in the reality of God's seventh-day creation festival. So Pieper is right on target when he goes on to assert that the man who is practicing leisure, who is living in the sabbath reality, "consents to his own true nature and abides in concord with the meaning of the universe."[5] These are marvelous ways of expressing the rich and complex joy of the Christian life that delves ever deeper into the mind-stretching truth of God, that strives with grace-driven zeal for more vibrant expressions of his goodness, and that sees with expanding awareness the beauty that God unfolds all around. This is the truth of the universe in which God's people graciously abide. This is the creation that the Christian does not flee but into which he leaps with happy abandon.

To live fully in concord with the creation, to be steeped in it, as we have learned, is not only about the festival and the celebration. It is also about doing what you have been given to do each day. It is about working. And it is also about joining in games and play and delighting in beauty all for their own sakes with no purpose beyond themselves. All of these are aspects of living as God calls us to live. To live in tune with God's intention

4 Josef Pieper, *Leisure: The Basis of Culture*, trans. Alexander Dru (San Francisco: Ignatius Press, 1952), 47.

5 Ibid., 48.

is to live with purpose, meaning, praise, and delight. To live with *purpose* is closely tied to our work; and to live with *meaning* is readily found in both our play and our love of beauty; and to live with *praise* correlates with the particular emphasis of leisure and worship; and finally, to live with *delight* is the all-encompassing purpose of sabbath. So it is that all the facets of life that we have considered in this book—purpose and work, meaning and beauty, praise and leisure, delight and sabbath—find their right places and their fullest expressions when seen together as complementary aspects of God's comprehensive, overall plan for his creatures.

It should come as no surprise to find Scripture concurring with the picture of the Christian life presented here. But what may be a bit unexpected is that some of the strongest support comes from the biblical book that repeatedly laments the pointlessness and the vanity of life. It is important to recall that Solomon's famous verdict of vanity is rendered when life is lived and evaluated apart from what God has revealed, and so the same teacher who can rightly cry, "Vanity of vanities!" can in the next breath offer worthy counsel for the conduct of life. Here are several instances that deserve careful attention:

> There is nothing better for a person than that he should eat and drink and find enjoyment in his toil. This also, I saw, is from the hand of God, for apart from Him who can eat or who can have enjoyment?
>
> What gain has the worker from his toil? I have seen the business that God has given to the children of man to be busy with. He has made everything beautiful in its time. Also, He has put

> eternity into man's heart, yet so that he cannot find out what God has done from the beginning to the end. I perceived that there is nothing better for them than to be joyful and to do good as long as they live; also that everyone should eat and drink and take pleasure in all his toil—this is God's gift to man.
>
> And I commend joy, for man has nothing better under the sun but to eat and drink and be joyful, for this will go with him in his toil through the days of his life that God has given him under the sun.
>
> Go, eat your bread with joy, and drink your wine with a merry heart, for God has already approved what you do. Let your garments be always white. Let not oil be lacking on your head. Enjoy life with the wife whom you love, all the days of your vain life that He has given you under the sun, because that is your portion in life and in your toil at which you toil under the sun. Whatever your hand finds to do, do it with your might, for there is no work or thought or knowledge or wisdom in Sheol, to which you are going.[6]

Notice how many of the themes and various threads of this book's discussion of work, leisure, and sabbath can be seen rooted in the words of Solomon. Work is God's gift to us, and

6 Ecclesiastes 2:24–25; 3:9–13; 8:15; 9:7–10, respectively (ESV).

those who are wise learn to delight in what God gives us to do. Vocation is not a burden to be solved but simply a matter of taking in hand what you see needs to be done and what you are able to do. Finding joy and delight in simple things and recognizing and contemplating the beauty built into the world and anchored in our hearts is key to living fully human lives. Joy, delight, and a merry heart are entirely appropriate outlooks for God's people. No doubt, a heavy undertone of the shortness of life and the weariness of living pervades all that Solomon writes, and he is right about that, of course. But, as people living in the fullness of God's grace, which is given abundantly in Christ, perhaps it is not wrong to suggest that as we are led by God's Spirit, we can follow the ancient king's faithful and wise counsel even more fully than he himself did. We know that the joy, the purpose, the meaning, and the wonder of life are not a passing fiction but are, in fact, the final reality; and one does not merely resign himself to make the most of things in a vain and bitter world. Rather, he rejoices to be God's creature in God's creation, which is on its way to a spectacular final consummation—the ultimate, perfect, eternal, sabbath celebration.

TODAY, THE VITA RECEPTIVA

Until then, we live as God calls us to live in the *vita receptiva*. God gives; we receive. All that we need he provides, even the vocational work and the play and the truth and the goodness and the beauty that make up our lives are gifts he provides. In his widely read work interpreting the Sermon on the Mount, Bonhoeffer captured wonderfully the power of the *vita receptiva* and the way it shapes every aspect of our thinking. Man does what God gives him to do, of course, but all the while he does it not for himself, and he does it knowing that God is the one who provides for him everything. Bonhoeffer describes, then, the thinking of the Christian who is living the *vita receptiva*:

> It is not worry, it is not even work which produces daily bread, but God the Father. The birds and the lilies do not work and spin, but they are fed and clothed; they receive their daily share without worry. They need the goods of the world only for daily life. They do not collect them. By not collecting they praise the creator, not by their industry, their work, their worry, but by receiving daily and simply the gifts God gives. That is how birds and lilies become examples for disciples. Jesus dissolves the connection between work and food, which is conceived in terms of cause and effect apart from God. He does not value daily bread as the reward for work. Instead, he speaks of the carefree simplicity of those who follow the ways of Jesus and receive everything from God.[7]

Creatures are dependent. They do not take care of themselves. God takes care of them. So we work not to meet our own personal needs—God lavishly takes care of every need we have purely by his gracious giving—we work to serve those around us. And we honor God and bring glory to him not by the great deeds we accomplish in our thinking, acting, or feeling but by doing what the birds do. We just receive. A daily unquestioning

7 Dietrich Bonhoeffer, *Dietrich Bonhoeffer Works*, vol. 4, *Discipleship*, eds. Geffrey B. Kelly and John D. Godsey, trans. Barbara Green and Reinhard Krauss (Minneapolis: Fortress Press, 2001), 166.

acceptance of everything God gives is the receptive life. And even this splendid way of life is itself one of the gifts given to us by God. So it is that we Christians live the receptive life; we live outside ourselves—in faith toward God and in love toward our neighbor. This is the "down and out" life. Grace and gifts come down to us as God delivers them. The neighbor then receives our works and service from us. God matters. The neighbor matters. We do not matter.

But that is a scandalous notion. Born already saturated in original sin and thoroughly self-obsessed by default, and then relentlessly tutored by our Western Enlightenment world to cultivate and perfect our base instinct for self-centeredness, people balk and bristle at the notion that they do not matter. But the idea of living outside of oneself, freely receiving and then freely giving, does lead inexorably in an altogether unusual direction and advances to a staggering conclusion. If we take the premise of the receptive life seriously, as we ought, the Christian is compelled to concede that he himself is unimportant. Orthodox theology will go so far as to endorse and encourage the necessity of the *odium sui*—yes, yet another superb Latin phrase; this one means the hatred of self. No doubt, hatred of self likely sounds quite dramatic and not only counter-intuitive but unkind and even ridiculous as it violates all of our Western culture's inviolable, indeed sacred, "truths" expressed in terms of self-love, self-respect, self-esteem, self-care, self-promotion, self-confidence, self-pride, self-preservation, and on and on with a vast litany of selfs. Nevertheless, in direct contradiction to this endorsement of the priority of self, Christian doctrine unapologetically declares the need for *odium sui*, which is but a pointed way of telling a person to see herself the right way.

This doctrine has solid grounding in Scripture. St. Paul offers a similar admonition to the Romans: "For through the grace given to me I say to everyone among you not to think more highly of himself than he ought to think; but to think so as to have sound judgment, as God has allotted to each a measure of faith." And he urged the Philippians, "Do nothing from selfishness or empty conceit, but with humility of mind regard one another as more important than yourselves; do not merely look out for your own personal interests, but also for the interests of others."[8] And Jesus' own exhortation clinches the argument: "If anyone wishes to come after Me, he must deny himself, and take up his cross and follow Me. For whoever wishes to save his life will lose it; but whoever loses his life for My sake will find it."[9] Dying to self means agreeing with God's judgment against sinners and so against yourself; it means learning to quit worrying about advancing your own agenda; it means learning to put everyone else ahead of yourself; in other words, it means learning to hate self. *Odium sui* is the fullest expression of the receptive life.[10]

Oddly and importantly, however, the *odium sui*, or the hatred of self understood in terms of the faithful expression of orthodox theology, is not the same thing as self-loathing. While in ordinary usage the two terms could rightly be considered as synonyms, in the world of right doctrine, *odium sui* and self-loathing are altogether different, indeed antithetical, things. The whole point of *odium sui* as a doctrinal truth is to forget about self in the delight of receiving from God and giving

8 Romans 12:3 and Philippians 2:3–4, respectively. It's worth noting that most translations of the text from Philippians considerably soften the Greek, which declares flatly: "Do not look out for your own things, but for the things of others."

9 Matthew 16:24–25.

10 For those interested in exploring the doctrinal aspects of *odium sui* a bit more, a great place to start is with the discussion of Luther's theology in Regin Prenter's *Spiritus Creator,* trans. John M. Jensen (Eugene: Wipf & Stock, 1953). See especially pages 4–13.

to the neighbor. It is not a grudging, morose, bitter activity or one overflowing with regret, sorrow, and loss. The opposite is true. Following the teaching of Jesus and his church and walking the path of dying to self leads one not to grief but to joy. Self-loathing is the polar opposite of *odium sui*. Initially it might seem that in self-loathing, the self has been denigrated or dismissed altogether, but in fact the reverse is true. The individual filled with self-loathing remains fully and wantonly immersed in the cult of self and is unashamedly turned in on self—in fact, in the miserable self's despair and self-abnegation, it can see nothing else but itself. Whether accurately or not, the person trapped in self-loathing is preoccupied and overcome with its self-recriminations and self-disgust. The self is the object of every hopeless thought and every plaintive word and every crushing inaction. The one caught in self-loathing needs to learn to die to self and to receive the liberating gift of the receptive life. By God's grace, he must renounce his sinful self-loathing and embrace the blessing of *odium sui*. The distinction between self-loathing and *odium sui*, and then the unhesitating affirmation of *odium sui* as the foundation upon which all human thriving is built, is profound truth that our world could never conjure let alone accept, but such are the marvels that become manifest when theology rejects the path of human reason and instead follows God's revelation.

THE SABBATH REST REMAINS

Wholeheartedly embracing the *vita receptiva* is a marvelous way to live one's life. From the outset, this book has been an unapologetic effort to offer a compelling argument that will lead people not only to consider these ideas but to agree with them and to receive for themselves the rich joy of living this sabbath life. Living in God's sabbath rest, living the *vita receptiva*, is about so much more than finding solutions to questions about sabbath observances or meticulously trying to follow a set of legalistic rules for personal time management. Indeed, such an approach directly undermines true sabbath living. The *vita receptiva* is about gaining a right outlook on every single day and on every single moment of one's entire life and seeing it all in the context of gifts received and gifts given—in faith toward God and in love toward the neighbor.

This means that getting sabbath right is not about salvaging Sunday, or Saturday for that matter, from the rest of the week. And learning to keep sabbath is definitely not about learning to prioritize time for oneself to "recharge" for the week ahead; in fact, this is virtually the antithesis of sabbath. Getting sabbath right is also not essentially about learning how to make Sunday special or set apart or different than all the other days. Advice or encouragement along these lines is pretty typical in most discussions about the sabbath. And Christians may well benefit from heeding such counsel; they may determine that establishing such practices actually enhances their celebration of festival days like Sunday and sharpens their delight in living in sync with God the Creator and with his extraordinary creation on every day.[11] But one can also certainly live a life steeped in the creation and saturated in the sabbath rest of God without fastidiously establishing boundaries between Sunday and Monday and every other day of the week or circumspectly devising a

11 Among the vast literature available on this topic, one would do well to consult any of the following: Dorothy C. Bass, *Receiving the Day: Christian Practices for Opening the Gift of Time* (Minneapolis: Fortress, 2019); Marva J. Dawn, *Keeping the Sabbath Wholly: Ceasing, Resting, Embracing, Feasting* (Grand Rapids: Eerdmans, 1989); Norman Wirzba, *Living the Sabbath: Discovering the Rhythms of Rest and Delight* (Grand Rapids: Brazos, 2006).

life schedule with an ideal balance between work and rest and leisure and play and worship. Indeed, as I have tried to make clear in the preceding chapters, trying to create hard divisions between any of these things is not an effort that should overly concern Christians. Determining whether what they are doing at any given moment is work or play or worship or service or leisure or appropriate for a Sunday is not the point—and not an exercise that offers much benefit. The better approach is to celebrate all that God gives and gives you to do and to embrace each new day and the peculiar wonders, joys, and opportunities it brings.

Some of our days will be crowded with much work; others will be focused almost entirely on meals and gatherings and parties that are all about delighting in the blessings of worship or family or even games; and other days, perhaps most days, will be an interesting mixture of all of these things. Since work is part of the lives God has planned for us, we have seen that work is an essential part of living the receptive life, which means it is an essential part of living in God's sabbath. So, work belongs with sabbath. And worship and play and games and leisure, or scholia, and all the other aspects of this life as God planned it for his human creatures also belong with sabbath. Living the receptive life is essentially about learning to live outside oneself—receiving and giving, and then finding delight in the very actions and processes involved in simply doing all the things that make up our lives. Working hard for the sake of others by fulfilling your vocational responsibilities is part of the receptive life, no doubt. But so is spending a day at a water park with your family, an al fresco dinner with friends, a competitive game of pickleball with coworkers, or walking with your spouse through your neighborhood. There is no established hierarchy or implicit ranking that necessarily asserts the priority of any one of these events over another; they are all equally important and delightful facets of the receptive life.

Our lives overflow with so many events big and small, routine and special, planned and spontaneous: changing a grandchild's diaper, barbecuing in the backyard with friends, preparing a bed for a vegetable garden, building a campfire for a long evening talking politics and church and philosophy, driving all day for a family vacation on the beach, devoting a morning to getting the meter just right in a poem, swinging on the porch and listening to the mesmerizing din of the spring peepers, going to the required campus chapel service to sing Matins with the student body, making tea for your spouse, or studying a flock of ten thousand blackbirds swooping and swirling en masse as evening approaches and then researching to learn more. Any of the items in this list might be work or play or leisure or worship. Does the difference matter? Why should we privilege some things with a particular lofty or respectable designation when all of these are simply activities that make up the lives of people living in tune with God's purpose and plan for his human creatures? All of these parts of life along with all true, good, and beautiful activities fit in the receptive life. They all belong in sabbath living. The wise creature learns to rejoice in each opportunity that is given and then delights in every single one as a delightfully different aspect of what it means to be human—both receiving and also giving exactly as God intends. The point of sabbath rest, the point of the receptive life, is living the life God gives and doing it the way he intends; and that means learning to delight in and savor all that he gives now and all that he will give forever.

the reason for we live the Down & Out Life

Delighting in the Down Out Life

Day 7: Embracing God's Sabbath and Gi
work, rest, or Pl
Re-thinking Sab

Joy fully living
Down and Out
Life and the Joy
it Brings

Gift & Plan
Design for the Down and Out Life

Sabbath and the
of Existence

The Point of it All

Your Reason for

Sabbath Work: Re-Thinking
Rest

God's Plan for

Receiving God